# ARCHERY
## FOR BEGINNERS

# ARCHERY
## FOR BEGINNERS

### The COMPLETE GUIDE to SHOOTING RECURVE and COMPOUND BOWS

AMANTE P. MARIÑAS, SR.

TUTTLE Publishing
Tokyo | Rutland, Vermont | Singapore

Published by Tuttle Publishing, an imprint of Periplus Editions (HK) Ltd.

**www.tuttlepublishing.com**

Copyright © 2019 Amante P. Mariñas, Sr.

Library of Congress Control Number: 2018965819

ISBN 978-0-8048-5153-4

DISTRIBUTED BY

*North America, Latin America & Europe*
Tuttle Publishing
364 Innovation Drive
North Clarendon, VT 05759-9436 U.S.A.
Tel: 1 (802) 773-8930
Fax: 1 (802) 773-6993
info@tuttlepublishing.com
www.tuttlepublishing.com

*Japan*
Tuttle Publishing
Yaekari Building, 3rd Floor
5-4-12 Osaki, Shinagawa-ku
Tokyo 141 0032
Tel: (81) 3 5437-0171
Fax: (81) 3 5437-0755
sales@tuttle.co.jp
www.tuttle.co.jp

*Asia Pacific*
Berkeley Books Pte. Ltd.
3 Kallang Sector #04-01,
Singapore 349278
Tel: (65) 6741 2178
Fax: (65) 6741 2179
inquiries@periplus.com.sg
www.tuttlepublishing.com

25 24 23 22 21
10 9 8 7 6 5 4 3 2

Printed in Malaysia     2102VP

TUTTLE PUBLISHING® is a registered trademark of Tuttle Publishing, a division of Periplus Editions (HK) Ltd.

## "Books to Span the East and West"

**Tuttle Publishing** was founded in 1832 in the small New England town of Rutland, Vermont [USA]. Our core values remain as strong today as they were then—to publish best-in-class books which bring people together one page at a time. In 1948, we established a publishing office in Japan—and Tuttle is now a leader in publishing English-language books about the arts, languages and cultures of Asia. The world has become a much smaller place today and Asia's economic and cultural influence has grown. Yet the need for meaningful dialogue and information about this diverse region has never been greater. Over the past seven decades, Tuttle has published thousands of books on subjects ranging from martial arts and paper crafts to language learning and literature—and our talented authors, illustrators, designers and photographers have won many prestigious awards. We welcome you to explore the wealth of information available on Asia at **www.tuttlepublishing.com**.

To my grandchildren Nadia & Amante III and
to my beloved wife Cherry

# ACKNOWLEDGMENTS

Thanks to my students, Stefan Dodson for the compound bow, Christopher Squires for the recurve bow, Stan Hubbard for the 550 paracord and freshly cut wood from his backyard, Ueli Laeng for the work he did on the rattan pole and on the anahaw, and to Thoraya Zedan for posing for the photographs, speed detector, and computer help.

Thanks to my valued family friends Glen and Babet Sullivan for the bamboo, to my son Amante II and daughter-in-law TaShana for the recurve bow, and to my wife Cherry who always had given me all the time I needed to put my thoughts into written words.

# CONTENTS

# PREFACE

I had plenty of practice with the slingshot having lived my childhood in a small village, Pambuan, in Central Luzon in the Philippines. There, if I wanted fruit, I had to climb a tree and if I wanted a snack—mainly birds—I had to catch them myself, really, shoot it down.

One time, I was able to shoot down a bird in full flight. Try as I might, I was never able to repeat the feat. It was a lucky shot. I was not the best shot in the village. One of my friends was. When he aimed at a bird, it was as good as done.

Three other activities that occupied our time were throwing stones by the river, throwing sharpened sticks (*bagakays*) at banana stalks, and shooting bamboo blowguns (short *sumpits*). In my childhood, we considered these as games. To my forebears, it was training for survival.

I now live half a world away in Fredericksburg, Virginia. I still shoot a slingshot (homemade), shoot blowguns (made of aluminum), and throw not wood but knives (steel). There is one obvious similarity among all these activities: a projectile is propelled toward a target by the release of stored energy

- in the bent throwing arm and the twist of the body in throwing a knife
- in the compressed air held in the lungs in shooting the blowgun, and
- in the stretched rubber bands in using a slingshot

I have published books on the blowgun (*Blowgun Techniques*) and on knife throwing (*The Art of Throwing*). I have written an unpublished manuscript on the conceptual physics of the slingshot, I said to myself, "Why not write a book on shooting the bow?"

I would have taken up archery much earlier in life but some things got in the way, including my writing on other topics. I started shooting the bow 12 years ago and to date I have retrieved about 200,000 arrows from my targets, which is really not that much considering I have thrown knives about 1,500,000 times and shot the blowgun about 800,000 times.

My experience in my daily bow shoots started crowding other things in my mind. The load on my mind got heavier than the proverbial ton-of-bricks. So one night, I decided to lighten it a bit. I started writing this book.

I shoot the bow daily, aiming to get to the 300,000-shot mark. Normally I shoot the bow early in the morning but sometimes I have to wait for the early morning robins to fly away after they had their fill of worms. I leave them alone. They have to eat and feed their young.

I merely want to hone my martial arts skills and have fun.

# INTRODUCTION

Recreational archery is one of the most popular pastimes in the country and for good reason. While there is a learning curve involved, as well as equipment you must purchase, the benefits to taking on archery are great.

So, what do you need to succeed in archery? Obviously, a healthy set of hands (and fingers) is critical if one is to become an archer. Safety is a very important part of succeeding in archery. From the earliest days, injuries and wounds afflicted archers. Today, archery is a sport and a pastime but in the past archery was a matter of life and death.

In the battle of Shrewsbury in 1403, a sixteen year old prince was hit by an arrow on the left side of his nose. He survived the wound but was left with permanent scars. Hence, he knew that archers were very much feared and hated by the enemy. Twelve years later, October 25, 1415, that prince, as King Henry V, led his army at the Battle of Agincourt. Just before the battle, in a speech to encourage his men he said, "...The French had boasted that they would cut two fingers of the right hand of all the archers that should be taken prisoners." The French lost the battle. Thus originated the "Agincourt salute" where the English and Welsh archers demonstrated that they didn't lose their bow fingers by flashing the two-finger "V" sign. Today, the stakes are not so high but the importance of avoiding injury is just as great.

You need, as well, a good bow, straight arrows, some accessories, and space. So you do need to spend some money to get the necessary tackle. But let us look at what you will get in return.

- Shooting the bow can improve your posture. You can't slouch and shoot the bow and expect to hit a target.
- Shooting the bow can be good exercise because it requires walking to retrieve your arrows. You can also use this time for other purposes as well. In my case, I meditate during the walk. Sometimes, I even practice martial arts moves. You can actually use this time to your advantage however you please.
- Shooting the bow can help develop patience. It is true that archery can be frustrating. If you miss the bull's-eye, try again. Your target will still be there the next day.
- Shooting the bow can be exhilarating—when you hit the bull's-eye, that is.
- Shooting the bow can make you aware of your surroundings helping you to become more safety conscious.

- Shooting the bow can helps develop a sense of care. If you are serious about archery, you will develop a habit of keeping your tackle (equipment) in good repair. This can translate to the care you take when using other things in your daily life.
- Shooting the bow can be a valuable mental exercise. You may not realize it, but subconsciously, you are solving mathematical equations when you shoot by intuition. When you shoot from 20 yards, you aim the arrowhead and hold it at a certain elevation. When you shoot from 25 yards, you change the elevation of your shot. Thus, shooting the bow can sharpen your sense of distance.
- Shooting the bow can help develop your ability to concentrate, if only for a few seconds. With each arrow you release, your mind is totally focused on the target.
- Shooting the bow can help you accept failure along with enjoying success. In archery, you can hit your shot perfectly or not. Every time you shoot, it is a challenge.
- Shooting the bow can teach humility. You may hit the bull's-eye with one shot and follow that up by missing the outermost circle. The constant ups and downs can help keep your ego in check.

When you shoot your first arrow, three things can happen: you can miss the target entirely, your arrow can hit somewhere inside the target, or you hit the bull's-eye. Your expression can range from "Aw, shucks!" to "I am good!" to "I am great!" It could take several thousand shots to get from "Aw, shucks!" to "I am good!" It could take thousands of shots to get to "I am great!" While progressing will be a slow and sometimes frustrating process, you are going to have fun!

Set modest goals. Along the way, you will hit the bull's-eye. Many times, you will miss. But what is the point of shooting the bow if you always hit a perfect shot? Ultimately, whatever you spend on your tackle will buy hours and hours of healthy mental and physical exercise.

# PART I: Archery Tackle

## CHAPTER 1

# THE BOW

In the past, archery was not a pastime or a sport. It was practiced as a means of war or as a means to obtain food. Because of this, bows were developed for very specific needs. The earliest bows were made using one piece of flexible wood, with a rigid middle bent at each end to the same degree, joined by a string made from natural fibers, sinew, silk, or rawhide. Modern bows are made of composite materials that complement each other's properties: one strong in tension; the other strong in compression.

Bows can be short or long. In the past, Native Americans used short bows for hunting while English archers used longbows. Hunters with short bows stalked their quarry and took aim from close range. Longbow archers stayed as far away as possible from their targets—they didn't have to aim. The archer merely pointed the arrow in the general direction of a crowd of enemies and let fly. Today, bow design is based on the bows of the past but with modern technology at its core.

There are 3 main types of bows:

⦿ Recurve bows—where the tips of the limbs point away from the archer and the string touches the bow before it is looped on the bow nocks.

⦿ Compound bows—which have much stiffer limbs than either those of the recurve or longbow. They use a system of pulleys (cams) and cables that transfers the applied pull to the limbs.

⦿ Straight bows—oftentimes called the longbow, where the tip of the limbs point toward the archer and where the string does not touch the bow except at the bow nocks (notches).

Because the recurve and the compound are the two most popular types of bows used in recreational archery by far, I cover them in this book.

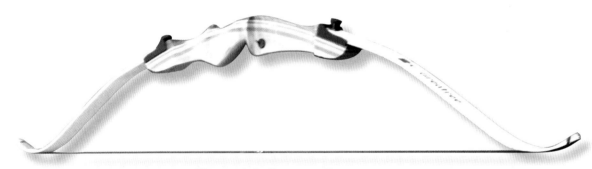

**Figure 1-1: Recurve Bow**

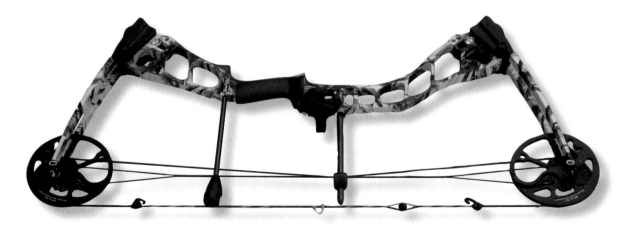

**Figure 1-2: Compound Bow**

The simple structure of the recurve (Figure 1-1) compared to the complexity of the compound bow (Figure 1-2) is immediately apparent.

# The Recurve Bow

The name "recurve" comes from the shape of the bow—the tips of the limbs of the recurve bow curve toward the target which gives the bow more power. The modern recurve is usually a takedown bow—its limbs can be replaced with limbs that have a lighter or a heavier draw weight—while older recurves are one-piece bows. The recurve is the only type of bow used in the Olympics.

The recurve consists of the riser, two limbs, and the bowstring. The riser is generally made of laminated wood, plastic, carbon, magnesium alloy, or aluminum alloy. The limbs are made of multiple layers of fiberglass with carbon and/or wooden core.

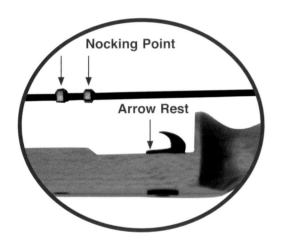

**Figure 1-3:** The string nocks of the recurve is equivalent to the nocking loop in the compound bowstring. When a release aid is used, it is clipped to the nocking loop. In a compound bow, the arrow is encircled by the arrow rest. In the recurve, the arrow is cradled by the arrow rest.

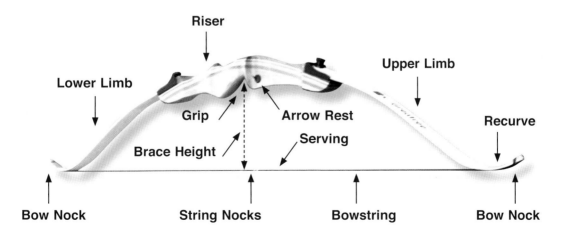

**Figure 1-4:** The takedown recurve is designed for ease of transport and interchangeability. A sight and a stabilizer can be attached to the riser.

The recurve bow is measured by its string length and weight. For example, a 62"/32 lbs. recurve bow has a 62" string length, measured from bow nock to bow nock (notches). The notches are where the ends of the bow strings are looped. The 32 lbs. indicates the amount of pull exerted on the string that will propel the arrow, not how much the bow weighs.

## Cost

If you want to buy a left-handed takedown recurve, shooting glove, safety goggles, stringer, forearm guard, quiver, and a dozen 500 spine arrows you could be spending around $300. It seems expensive but it isn't really. The recurve will last many years. For a bow that lasts 10 years, this amounts to spending $30 a year. It will cost you more than $30 to see one movie and have dinner afterward with a friend. (The recurve is listed at 28 lbs. weight but it feels more like 35 lbs. If you are not comfortable with the weight of a recurve do not hesitate to return it.)

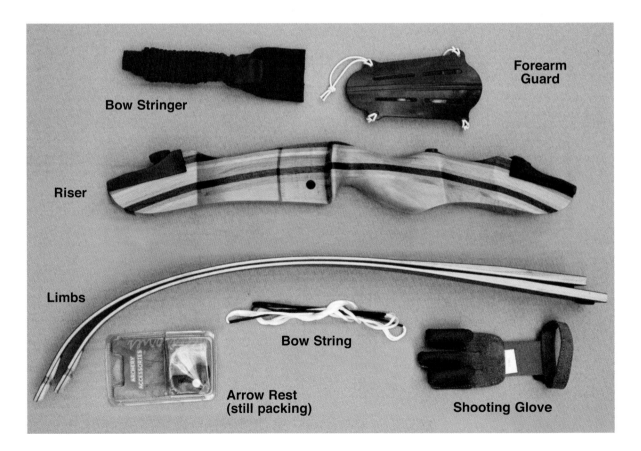

**Figure 1-5:** If you ordered your bow online, it will come unassembled. You do not need any tools to assemble the recurve. However, if you have not used a bow before, you might need help stringing it. You can follow the instructions here or you can easily find instructions online. (Courtesy Thoraya Zedan)

Of course, you can opt for a more expensive bow. However, just because you buy a more expensive bow does not mean that you will become a more accurate shooter. The more accurate archer is the one who shoots with consistently proper form.

## Draw Weight

Typically, the average draw weight of a bow is between 35 and 45 lbs. for men and between 20 and 35 lbs. for women. If you are an adult male or female, a 35 lbs. or even a 32 lbs. bow will be good weights to shoot where you have limited space, such as in a backyard. There is increased risk of damage to property shooting more powerful bows.

I have a student who had been studying with me for more than 12 years. One time, he brought his bow to class. I asked him to shoot one arrow. It took quite an effort for him to draw to his anchor point. I nocked an arrow and tried to draw the bowstring. I couldn't get my string arm to my anchor point. My student was over bowed. It was even worse for me.

You cannot shoot properly if you are over bowed. You will be overbowed when your string hand starts shaking at your anchor point and when you spray the target with your arrows. You will struggle to draw to your anchor point and as a result you are going to tire quickly. Your draw should be relaxed and comfortable so that you can focus on your aim.

If you had not handled a bow before, it is better to start with a bow that you can pull easily. This way, you can concentrate on developing good form rather than struggling to get to the full draw.

If you do, you will benefit in a number of ways.

- You can shoot many arrows one after the other without feeling fatigued.
- You will be shooting safely.
- You will avoid self-inflicted injury.
- Over time, you will build up your muscles and get stronger.
- You will have fun.

Later, you can try a recurve with the next higher draw weight. If you have a 1-piece recurve, you have to get another recurve. If you have a takedown recurve, you can usually get heavier limbs. I pull a recurve with a modest draw weight. I am able to shoot 200 arrows and not feel physically fatigued. However, mental fatigue usually sets in after shooting that many arrows.

**Figure 1-6:** The recurve comes in different lengths and weights.

## Center Shot

Most modern bows are made with the center shot design. The center shot is not a particular spot. It is the cut out section in the bow's upper limb at the handle that causes the arrow to point straight ahead when the string is drawn. Traditional Japanese and Chinese bows, for example, don't have a center shot design so the drawn arrow points to one side.

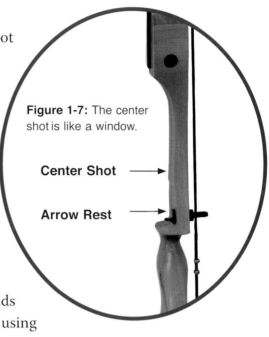

**Figure 1-7:** The center shot is like a window.

**Center Shot** ⟶

**Arrow Rest** ⟶

## Draw Length

One of the ways of determining the archer's draw length is by measuring the distance between the tips of the middle fingers of the outstretched hands then dividing the measure by 2.5. My draw length using this method is 67/2.5 = 27".

**Figure 1-8:** An easy way to measure draw length is by measuring the distance between your middle fingertips.

Of course, there is no substitute for determining the draw length by pulling the bowstring to the anchor point then marking the arrow 1" past the arrow rest. The distance of that mark to the bowstring at your anchor point is another way of measuring your draw length.

The archer's draw length must be consistent. For example: If I pull the bowstring to 27" and if I aimed correctly, I will hit the bull's-eye. If I pull the bowstring to 26½" and release the arrow, my arrow will hit low.

For consistency, the recurve archer can use a clicker. A clicker is a device that clicks when the archer reaches his optimum draw length. When you hear the click, simply stop pulling and release the arrow.

## Stringing the Recurve

The bow can be stringed or unstringed by hand or with the help of a bow stringer. To string the bow by hand:

**Figure 1-9:** Anchoring the curved lower end.          **Figure 1-10:** Bending the upper end.

- Loop the lower end of the string around the lower notch of the bow.
- Hold the upper end of the string in your left hand and the bow's upper end with your right hand.
- Step with your right foot between the lower limb and the bowstring.
- Anchor the curved lower end against your left ankle. This will put the riser against the back of your right leg (Figure 1-9).
- Bend (push to the front) the bow's upper end with your right hand and slip the loop on the notch (Figure 1-10).

The procedure to unstring the bow is essentially the same except that of removing the loop from the notch. Unstring the bow after you shoot or if it is to be stored indefinitely. However, if you shoot everyday, stringing and unstringing your bow could become a chore even if you use a bow stringer.

**Figure 1-11:** Even with a bow stringer, you might need help in stringing or unstringing the recurve if you have short hands. (Courtesy Thoraya Zedan)

# The Compound Bow

The ideal place to get a compound bow is from an archery shop. You can receive personalized assistance there to help you determine your draw length (which determines the length of the arrow you can shoot) and the draw weight that fits your physical make-up. The staff there will even adjust the draw length and the draw weight of the compound bow for you. At the same time that you get your bow, you should get the matching arrows and accessories to complete your tackle.

An archery shop also might have a shooting range. If it does, the resident shop pro will be only too happy to let you loose some arrows for practice. This will be a good time to experience what is called "let off" (see page 26).

## Parts of the Compound Bow

The many parts of the compound bow can look intimidating. The most important parts you should be familiar with are as follows. Other useful accessories are covered in Chapter 3.

- **Riser**—The riser of a compound bow is usually made of aluminum, magnesium alloy, or carbon fiber. It is the central component of the bow. The grip is on the riser. The limbs, cable rod, string suppressor, and accessories such as stabilizer, sight, and quiver are attached to the riser.
- **Limbs**—Limbs, made of fiber glass, are attached to the riser by limb bolts. Limbs store the energy as the bowstring is pulled.
- **Cams**—Elliptical cams are attached at the end of the lower and upper limbs. Cams can be draw length specific. Others can be adjustable that allow the archer to change the bow's draw length. The cables and bowstring are attached to the cams. The cams transfer the limbs' energy to the bowstring.
- **Cables**—Cables run between the cams and move the cams when the bowstring is pulled.
- **Cam system**—Also known as eccentrics. It consists of the cams and the cables that run between the cams.
- **Cable rod**—It is attached to the riser and on which is mounted the cable slide.
- **Cable slide**—This is mounted on the cable rod and through which is threaded the cables to keep the cables away from the path of the arrow.
- **Bowstring**—The bowstring is attached from one cam to the other. The bowstring[4] propels the arrow. It is normally made of high modulus polyethylene that had great tensile strength and has minimal stretchability. The compound bow is never unstrung. The bowstring has to be waxed.
- **String suppressor**—Absorbs the vibration of the bowstring.

**Figure 1-12:** Parts of the compound bow.

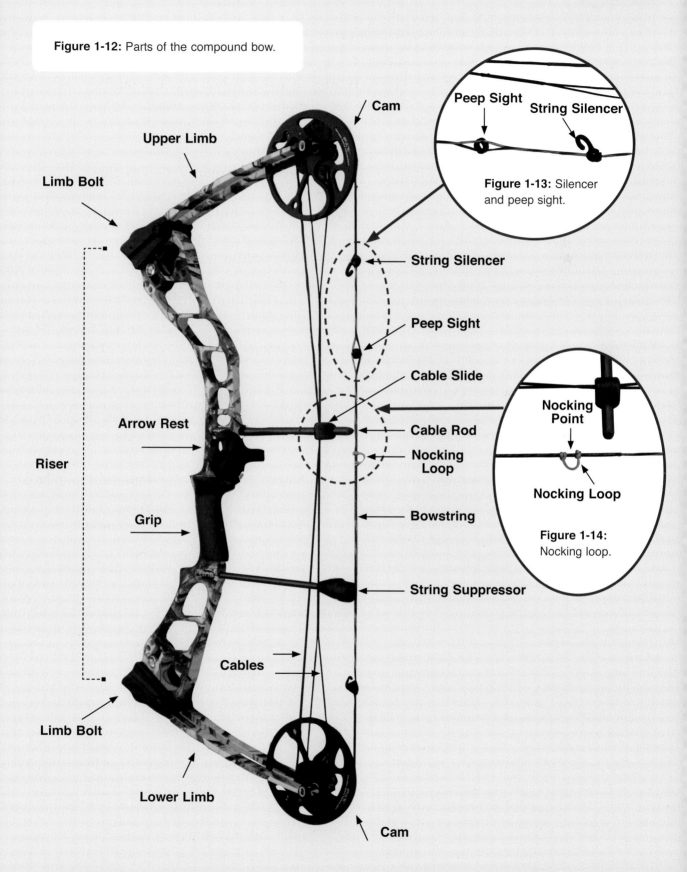

Cam

Upper Limb

Limb Bolt

**Figure 1-13:** Silencer and peep sight.

Peep Sight

String Silencer

String Silencer

Peep Sight

Cable Slide

Riser

Arrow Rest

Cable Rod

Nocking Point

Nocking Loop

Nocking Loop

Grip

Bowstring

**Figure 1-14:** Nocking loop.

String Suppressor

Cables

Limb Bolt

Lower Limb

Cam

## Cost

Compound bows are usually customized with a number of accessories already attached to the riser. The peep sight and string silencer (Figure 1-13) are attached to the bowstring. The release aid is clipped to the nocking loop (Figure 1-14). Accessories such as a stabilizer, release aid, and bow sight are designed to help the archer make accurate shots and would be good additions to your compound bow.

Because the compound bow has so many parts as well as extra accessories that an archer should have, it is quite expensive—more expensive than a recurve. The bow shown above (Figure 1-2), including five arrows, cost $407. A bow sight, quiver, and a stabilizer can easily add another $300 to the cost of the compound bow. You should definitely take this into account when making your decision on which bow to choose.

## Draw Weight

The draw weight of a recurve is specific. You can't adjust the draw weight of a recurve. On the other hand, that of a compound bow can be adjusted. The draw weight of a compound bow can be adjusted by turning the limb bolt counterclockwise using an Allen wrench. However, altering the bow's draw weight is complicated and is best left to the professional. A shop pro will start you with a low draw weight then work you up to your most comfortable draw weight.

Recreational archery is a form of mental and physical relaxation. Hence, your draw weight should be such that you are able to shoot over and over without getting fatigued. If you are over bowed, shooting the bow will not be fun—it will be a struggle.

## Draw Length

The bowstring of a recurve or a long bow can be drawn back as far as the archer's strength will allow. On the other hand, the bowstring of a compound bow can only be pulled back so far. The distance at which the draw stops is the compound bow's draw length. This draw length is determined by the cam systems of the bow. The bow's draw length is adjusted to fit the archer's draw length. Such a match will result in the best possible bow shot.

## Let Off

Compound bows come with single, dual, hybrid, and binary cams. Single cam compound bows are recommended for those who are just starting out on shooting a bow. Single cam compound bows have a round idler wheel at the top of the bow and an elliptical cam at the bottom. At some point, the turning of the cams results in what is called "let off."

In a recurve, it becomes more difficult to pull the bowstring as the draw progresses. It becomes most difficult at full draw. If the recurve is rated at, say, 50 lbs. at the end of the pull, at full draw, the archer will be holding 50 lbs. You will not be able to hold his aim for long and will have to release the arrow. In a recurve, there is no let off and you can pull the bowstring as far back as your strength and arm length will allow.

However, in a compound bow, a point is reached at near-full draw where the cam has turned to its full extent. At this time, the mechanical advantage gained kicks in and allows a reduced holding weight. This is the "let off" point. For example, if the draw weigh of a compound bow is 50 lbs. and has a designed 75% let off, the archer will be holding the equivalent of 12.5 lbs. at full draw. [Calculated as (1.0–0.75) x 50 = 12.5)]. The lower holding weight enables the archer to keep the full draw longer and allows more time to aim. This results in more accurate shots. The difference in holding weights is shown in Figure 1-18.

**Figure 1-15:** At the start of the draw.

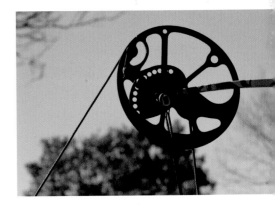

**Figure 1-16:** Just after the let off.

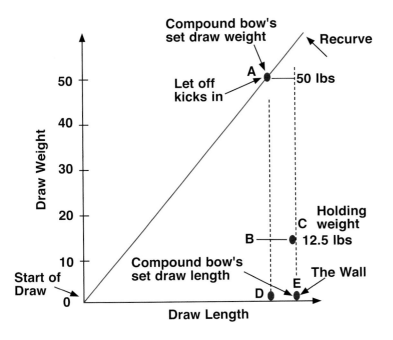

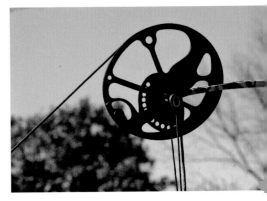

**Figure 1-17:** At the wall. Positions of the upper cam as the bowstring is pulled.

**Figure 1-18:** A representation of the drawing of a compound bow as the holding weight drops from 50 lbs. to 12.5 lbs. (Not to scale.)

**Figure 1-19:** Start of the draw.

**Figure 1-20:** Just before "let off" at peak draw weight.

When you nock the arrow then grip the bowstring, you would have exerted minimal effort on it practically zero (0). As you pull, the string pulls back with equal force. Eventually, you reach the peak 50 lbs. draw weight (point A) where your string hand will be at point D. The let-off kicks in. The 50 lbs. pull becomes a 12.5 lbs. holding weight (point C) and your string hand ends up at point E. This is when you hit the so called "wall" (point E). Drawing the string beyond the wall would require tremendous energy and will serve no purpose.

## Recurve vs. Compound

Which kind of bow is right for you, recurve or compound? You might choose one over the other based on appearance. Then, you would look at the bottom line—price. Say, you picked one, despite its price. What would you want to use it for? Hunting? Target practice?

I have shot them both and I would like to share my experience (based on 32 lbs. bows).

◉ The recurve is lighter, maybe, about half the weight of a compound bow. This matters because it is a heavy load on the bow arm (the arm that holds the bow). In my case, I can shoot ten arrows in a row with the recurve without feeling fatigued. On the other hand, I can only shoot three with the compound bow then I had to pause to rest my bow arm. I have no problem with my string arm pulling my draw weight with either bow.

**Figure 1-21:** Just after the let off.   **Figure 1-22:** At the wall. Positions of the string hand when shooting the compound bow.

- I can string and unstring the recurve without using any tools. You can't do the same with the compound bow.
- I have been able to replace or extend the useful life of some of the accessories of the recurve.
- I have to retrieve the arrows from my target. I have no problem laying down the recurve on its side anywhere. I can't do the same with the compound bow because of its many moving parts and its irregular shape. See Figure 1-2 above.
- The compound bow has many moving parts. Hence, there are more places where failures could occur. The first compound bow I had broke.
- The bowstring vibrations are dampened by the string suppressor. There is no such provision in the recurve bow.
- There is no "let off" in the recurve. The "let off" makes the compound bow unique.
- The compound bow is more expensive.

## Release Aid

A bow sight and a mechanical release aid are standard for the compound bow. It is optional for the recurve. I have shot the recurve with no sight attached and using a finger glove. I use the split finger grip on the bowstring. I did not use a release aid shooting the recurve. Hence, when I shoot the compound bow with no release aid, the muscle memory that I developed shooting the recurve gets carried over for the string fingers wouldn't know whether the bowstring is on a compound bow or on a recurve.

## Sight

The compound bow I shoot does not have a sight attached. Hence, I shoot it using instinctive shooting. I still look for a shooting configuration just like I do with my recurve and then I release the arrow. However, I had to make one adjustment.

In the beginning, I used a 28" arrow with my compound bow. However, the arrow rest completely covered the arrow head. Since, I have been shooting my recurve using 32" arrows, I had a ready substitute. It worked well. Now, I can see the arrow head beyond the arrow rest. But of course, it will be better if I replace the compound arrow rest with a recurve-type arrow rest.

## Optimum Draw Length

There is no need for a clicker for a compound bow. Once the let-off kicks in, the archer hits the wall. He can't pull the bowstring any further. Of course, he might make a mistake and relax his pull. In which case, the bowstring will move toward the front. He will feel the draw getting heavy again. The distance between the wall and the point where the draw starts to get heavy again is called the valley. A 0.5" valley is considered generous and wide enough for a beginning compound bow archer. See Figure 1-23.

The valley is not a built-in design. It is a result of the interaction between the cam system, the bow's limbs, and the bowstring. It is not that difficult to pull the bowstring back to the wall because of the light holding weight.

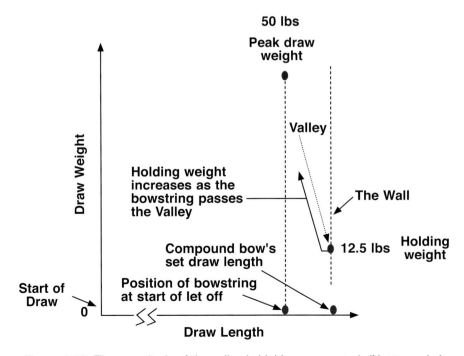

**Figure 1-23:** The magnitude of the valley is highly exaggerated. (Not to scale.)

## Strings

The recurve bowstring is made of Dacron (2.6% stretch, 50 lbs. strength per strand). Dacron has more stretch than the high modulus polyethylene (1% stretch, 100 lbs. strength per strand) used in the compound bow.

The lengths of the bowstring above and below the string nocks are not the same. In the recurve bow pictured (Figure 1-24) the bowstring above the nocking point is 29" while the length of the bowstring below the nocking point is 33". The 4" difference in lengths explains the great difference between the vibrations of the upper limb and that of the

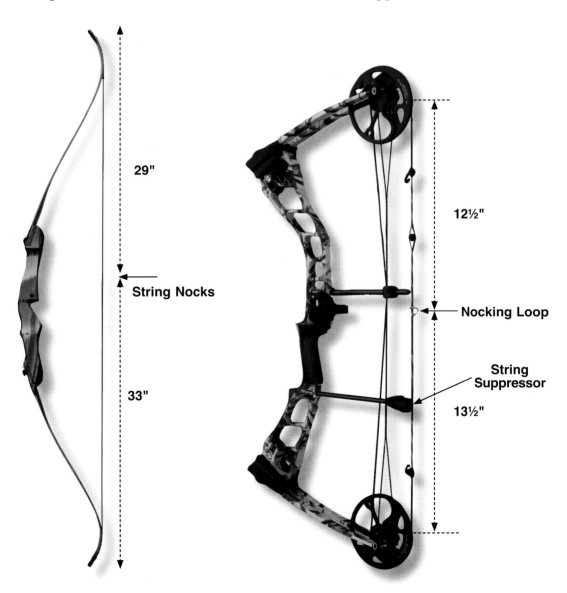

**Figure 1-24:** The placement of the string nocks on a recurve bow.

**Figure 1-25:** The placement of the nocking loop on a compound bow.

lower limb (Figure 1-26). The lower limb doesn't seem to be moving at all. One might take it for granted that the nocking point is at the middle of the recurve bowstring. It is not. The nocking point in the compound bowstring is not in the middle either. It is about 1" off center (Figure 1-25).

The draw weight is applied closer to the upper limb. Hence, when the string is released a lot more energy is transmitted to the upper limb. The 29" portion of the bowstring vibrates faster than the longer 33" inch portion. If you look closely at a much used recurve bowstring, the portion above the nocking point will look "fuzzier."

**Figure 1-26:** Shooting a recurve bow.

**Figure 1-27:** Shooting a compound bow.

The vibration of the upper limb of the recurve (Figure 1-26) is very pronounced compared to that of the compound bow (Figure 1-27) which looks like it didn't vibrate at all. This marked difference between the frequency and magnitude of the vibrations between the two bows is due to the string silencer, the rigid limbs, and the string suppressor. The rigid limbs minimize the vibrations. The weights of the two string silencers and the limited stretch (1%) of the bowstring resist the vibrations. The energy transferred from the bowstring to the string suppressor at impact further reduces the vibrations. The reduced vibration increases the archer's chances of hitting what he is aiming at.

Ultimately, I would suggest that, in order to make an informed choice, you take a trip to an archery shop. There is a good chance that they will have an archery range there. You can ask to shoot a few arrows from both bows in order to get an idea of how both bows feel to you.

CHAPTER 2

# THE ARROW

The arrow is the other half of a potentially deadly pair. Historically, the arrow was made from wood, bamboo, or other materials readily available. Bamboo bows and arrows were the most used in Asia. Native Americans use ash, birch, and other types of wood from which shafts can be made that are light, stiff, and straight.

Wooden arrows are still popular although they are liable to warp. Modern arrows are hollow and made from fiberglass, aluminum, or carbon. This author uses carbon arrows which he finds very durable.

## Arrow Length

The length of the arrow for a particular individual is determined by measuring the distance from the chest to the tip of the fingers (Figure 2-1); or by pulling the string to a full draw until the string hand reaches the anchor point then marking the arrow at a point 1" past the arrow rest.

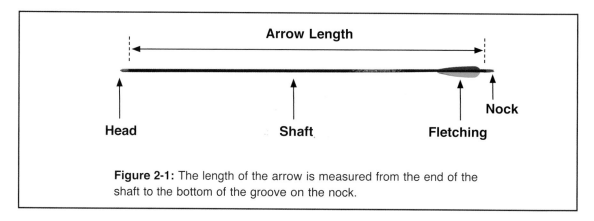

**Figure 2-1:** The length of the arrow is measured from the end of the shaft to the bottom of the groove on the nock.

In both cases I felt the arrow length was not long enough. Hence, in the second method, at full draw, I measured my arrow length from the bowstring to the tip of the knuckles of my bow arm then added 2 inches. The length I came up with was 31". I shoot 32" and 29" arrows.

**Figure 2-2:** The length of the arrow depends on the length of the bowman's arm. Instead of an arrow a ruler is used here.

In a sense I am "over arrowed." However, a longer, heavier arrow will not carry that far which is good for shooting in a backyard. It is better to have a longer arrow than a shorter one. If too short, the arrowhead could slide off the arrow rest and that would put your bow hand in front of it.

## Parts of the Arrow

The arrow consists of the head (or point), insert, shaft, fletchings, and nock. Arrows can come assembled and ready to shoot. Or, the parts can be bought separately then assembled into a whole.

**Arrowhead**—This comes in different shapes depending on whether it is to be used for hunting or target practice. It is screwed into the aluminum insert at the front end of the arrow.

**Insert**—This is an aluminum piece that is glued into the shaft to which the arrowhead is screwed in.

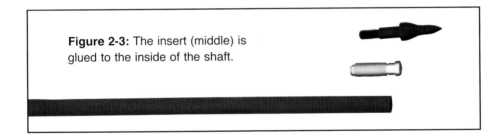

Figure 2-3: The insert (middle) is glued to the inside of the shaft.

**Shaft**—The shaft can be made of wood, aluminum, fiberglass, or carbon.

**Fletchings**—Fletchings can be feathers or plastic vanes and come in different colors and shapes and are equally spaced around the shaft. Two have a different color than the index fletching. One of the arrows I shoot has 2 greens and 1 orange. One other arrow I shoot has 2 whites and 1 green. The index fletching informs the archer how to orient the nock. The orange fletching serves one other purpose: it stands out in the grass and will help in finding the arrow that missed the "broad side of a barn."

**Nock**—The nock is made of a grooved plastic and inserted (pushed) into the other end of the shaft. When the arrow is nocked one is ready to pull the bowstring.

# Characteristics of a Good Arrow

Arrows must be straight, of uniform weight, and match the bow in stiffness. If these conditions are met and you have good shooting mechanics, you are going to get tight groups and high scores.

The qualities of the arrow are quantified with some number. For example: there is a measure for straightness and for stiffness. Uniform weight implies that each of the arrow's parts must have the same weight for all arrows.

The 32" carbon arrow I shoot with my recurve has a diameter of 0.281", straightness of 0.006" and with a 500 spine. The weights of the parts of the arrow are: shaft, 7.3 grains per inch (gpi); fletchings, 6 grains each; nock, 13 grains; and insert, 21 grains. The total weight of the arrow is 286 grains (about 18 grams). The recommended weight of the arrow is at least 5 grains per lbs. of draw weight.

**Material**—Shafts can be made of wood, aluminum, fiberglass, or carbon. Wood is affected by moisture and temperature, could bend, and lose its straightness.

Carbon arrows consist of an inner and an outer carbon tube. A Magnesium-Aluminum-Silicon fiber is twisted around the inner tube that enhances the arrow's flexibility. Carbon arrows stay straight even with prolonged use.

**Straightness**—Straightness range from .001" to .006". The smaller the number the straighter is the arrow and the more accurate it is to shoot.

**Weight**—The weight of the shaft is 7.3 gpi (grains per inch) and is one of two numbers imprinted on the arrows I use.

The weight of the shaft is the number that registers when it is put on a weighing scale. The weight of the bow 32 lbs. is the amount of pull. The amount of pull is lb.-force not lb.-weight. If I put a 32 lbs.-weight on your head, no harm will come to you. If I hit your head with a 32 lbs.-force, you will experience a giant headache. The 32-lbs. force is the energy applied to the bowstring and the bow is rated 32 lbs. weight.

**Stiffness**—The one other number imprinted on my arrow is 500. This is the resistance of the arrow to bending and is called static spine. Static spine is the amount of flex (bend) when a static load of 880 grams (1.94 lbs.) is suspended at the center of a 29" arrow with two supports ½" away from each end. Hence, an arrow that bends .500 inch off center has a static spine of 500. A smaller number indicates that the shaft will bend less. An arrow that has a 300 static spine is stronger than one that has a 500 static spine.

Another measure of stiffness is called dynamic spine. It is the deformation of the arrow as it is propelled from the bowstring. There is no numerical value for dynamic spine because it depends on many factors among which are the bow's draw weight, the weight of the arrow, weight of the inserts, method of release, and static spine.

Stiffness will determine the arrow's behavior as it is released and as it heads toward the target. If the arrow bends too little, it will veer away from the target; if enough, it will clear the center cut and will result in a good shot; if too much, it could shatter. For this reason, some arrows have an imprint like 40 lbs. max. This means that the arrow should not be used in bows of heavier weight, say, 50 lbs.

As an analogy, when you start going up in an elevator, you may feel your knees buckle from the unexpected and sudden acceleration. It is the same thing with the arrow. It will buckle as it is subjected to sudden acceleration.

## Selecting the Arrow

The arrow must match the bow. You do not have to figure this out yourself. On some maker's websites, you can find a shaft selector tool. You simply enter the type of bow (recurve, etc.) and the bow weight. Then you fill in arrow cut length, say 32". A screen will pop up showing the model name, spine, size, weight (grains per inch), and straightness of the arrow that is matched to your bow.

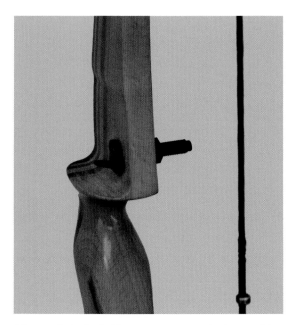

**Figure 2-4:** A pliable arrow rest made from rubber.

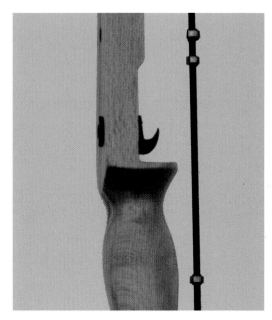

**Figure 2-5:** A rigid arrow rest made from plastic.

You can also get this information at an archery shop where you buy the right arrows that will match your bow. In a warehouse store that sells everything and the kitchen sink, sales associates will probably not be able to offer expert help. You will have to know what you are looking for.

If you buy arrows on the Internet, make sure that they are "ready to shoot." Otherwise, you could receive a package that will contain only shafts and inserts. Then, separately, you have to buy arrowheads, fletchings, glue, and nocks. You will have to assemble the parts. Gluing the fletchings to the shaft is not something easily learned.

Arrow rests could be either made of hard plastic or something pliable. The arrow must match the bow. One seemingly trivial thing is that the vanes of the arrow must be compatible with the arrow rest.

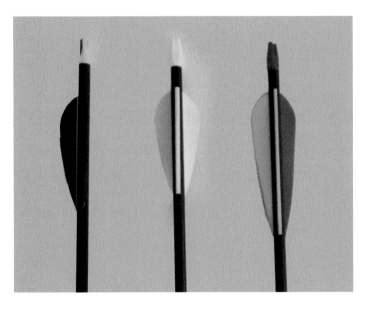

**Figure 2-6:** The arrow at left is feather-like. In the two other arrows, the vanes are single pieces. The feather-like arrow is better suited to be shot from a bow that has a hard plastic arrow rest (Figure 2-5).

**Figure 2-7:** The vanes are not a continuous piece as can be seen in the parted barbs of the black fletching.

CHAPTER 3

# ACCESSORIES

You are now ready to shoot. However, you need a shooting glove or finger tab to protect your string fingers and a bow arm guard to protect the inside of your (bow) forearm. These are all the accessories you need for instinctive shooting. Other accessories will help improve your shooting scores such as the bow sight, stabilizer, clicker, and kisser.

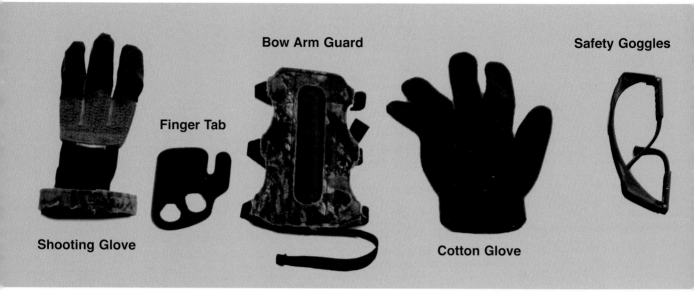

**Figure 3-1:** Accessories (left to right): shooting glove, finger tab, bow arm guard, cotton glove, and safety goggles.

**Shooting glove**—This is a leather glove that protects the three string fingers from repeated abrasions as the arrow is released. If you use a release aid, you will not need a shooting glove. I prefer the shooting glove over the finger tab. One of my shooting gloves lasted 63,805 shots.

**Finger tab**—The finger tab is made of leather worn over and protects the string fingers. The finger tab that came with my recurve bow has small holes that I had to enlarge to fit my fingers.

**Bow arm guard**—A strap of leather or canvas topped with hard plastic that protects the inside of the forearm from the whipping motion of the bow string. If you shoot in warm weather in short sleeves, it is good practice to use it. A long-sleeved jacket will serve the purpose in cold weather.

**Cotton glove**—A callus could form on the knuckle of the thumb of the bow hand depending on the number of arrows you shoot. If you shoot only during weekends or occasionally, you will not need the glove. I shoot at least 100 arrows daily. The callus could become thick and annoying. For this reason, I wear a tight fitting glove in my left (bow arm) hand to prevent the callus from getting too thick. I use the cotton glove sparingly during the hot months.

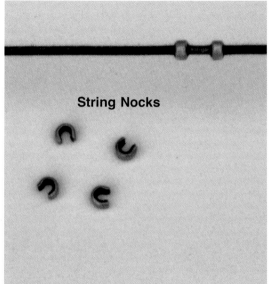

**String Nocks**

**Figure 3-2:** String nocks.

**Figure 3-3:** A Venetian blind box (reinforced with duct tape at the top) can be used as a quiver. This particular "quiver" lasted more than ten years. It got rained on and I replaced it with a quiver made from bamboo.

**Safety goggles**—I had two operations on both my eyes. For this reason, I wear safety goggles to guard against the possible breaking of the bow string or the breaking of the arrow shaft. Safety goggles are necessary when shooting the compound bow because the bow could shatter and could send broken fragments toward the archer.

**String nocks**—Nocks are C-shaped pieces made of brass placed in pairs on the bowstring between which the arrow is notched. The string you buy to replace one that broke will not come with string nocks attached. You have to place them on the string.

To attach the string nocks lay down an arrow on the arrow rest perpendicular to the string. (A T-square will be of great help. Or you can line up the edge of a ruler with the bowstring.) Nock the arrow on the string then mark the proper location of the string nocks. Use a pair of pliers to close their ends and check that they are secure. The string nocks ensure that an arrow is nocked in the same place (nocking point) in every shot.

**Quiver**—The quiver is used to carry arrows. You may purchase a quiver or craft one of your own. My quiver is an empty Venetian blind box that I recline on a chair. This "quiver" works well with me because I shoot only in my backyard.

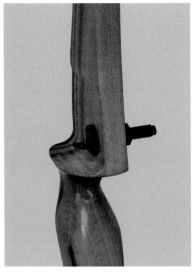

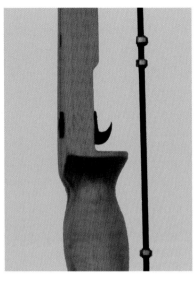

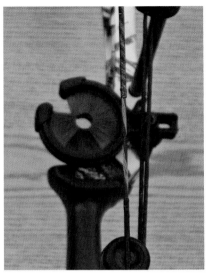

**Figure 3-4:** A recurve right handed arrow rest.

**Figure 3-5:** A recurve left handed arrow rest.

**Figure 3-6:** A compound arrow rest.

**Arrow rests**—Arrow rests help stabilize the arrow as you aim. They are beneficial for steady shooting for both beginner and experienced archers alike.

**Bow sight**—An aiming device attached to the bow. I use instinctive shooting a style of shooting that does not use a bow sight.

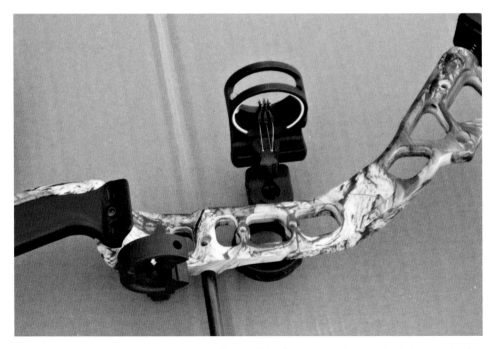

**Figure 3-7:** Compound bow with sight attached.

**Bow press**—A mechanical device that presses the compound bow's limbs toward the center that releases the tension on the bowstring and cables. It is used for maintenance and to string the compound bow. The compound bow is too expensive and too complicated to fiddle with. If your string breaks, it is best to go to an archery shop and let the pros do it. You can also check the warranty on your bow that will point you to a dealer who would do it for you.

These are discussed in detail in later chapters.

You now have the bow, arrow, and accessories. You are ready to shoot. However, before you do so, you should understand
- That pain or discomfort usually accompany a physical activity
- That there is need for warm up exercises
- The factors that could affect your ability to hit a target
- The concept of instinctive shooting
- The process of aiming

**Bow stringer**—Essentially a rope used to string or unstring a recurve bow. A bow press is needed to string or unstring a compound bow.

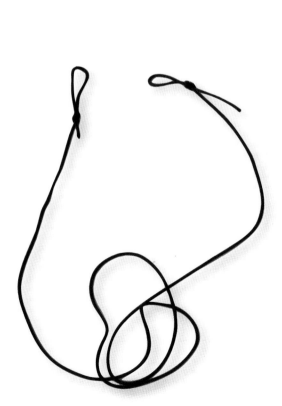

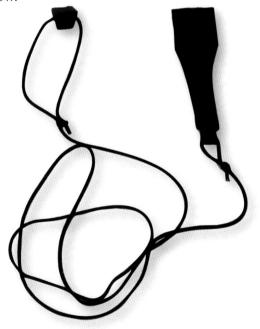

**Figure 3-8:** At left is a homemade bow stringer; at right, a commercial bow stringer. If the bow stringer is longer than is necessary, tie a knot in the middle to make it shorter.

CHAPTER 4

# CARE OF YOUR TACKLE

You should be diligent in keeping your tackle (equipment) in good working order. In this way, the only cause of an errant shot will be your aim. Keep a spare recurve bow string and an arrow rest to ensure that you always have them on hand when you are shooting. Because compounds bows are more complex, you may have to take a trip to the closest archery shop to have them replace the bowstring and the arrow rest.

Damage to your bow can be prevented. **First and foremost, never dry fire your bow!** It is particularly dangerous to dry fire a compound bow. It could shatter scattering sharp fragments towards the archer as well as others in the area. So, in this way, caring for your tackle will not only help you shoot better but it will also help you shoot safer.

Damage to arrows can be prevented and minimized in a number of ways.

1. Use a target that has more than one circle—If the circles are small shoot only one arrow at each circle.
2. Use a big target—There are less chances of hitting already embedded arrows when shooting at a big target.
3. Shoot only a limited number of arrows even at a big target.
4. Use a soft target.
5. Use at least eight layers of cardboards to prevent the arrow from penetrating too deep.

Shooting only one arrow at one circle then retrieving it will entail a lot of walking particularly if you shoot one hundred times. For example: If you shoot one hundred arrows in groups of four, you will make twenty five round trips to retrieve them before you can shoot again. If your target is fifty steps away, you will walk a total of 2,500 steps. However, it is a good trade off: a slowed learning versus getting rid of some calories.

**Mow your lawn**—Maintaining your lawn is less about maintenance of your tackle than it is about avoiding loss of arrows. Occasionally, you will make a very bad shot and will completely miss the target. If the grass in your lawn is more that 6 inches tall, it will not be easy to find the arrow. If the arrow has a glow-in-the-dark nock, you will have to wait until it gets dark to find it. You can also use a metal detector. In the meantime, the lost arrow becomes mental clutter and will not help your aim. Most important, it is not safe to mow your lawn with a lost arrow in the grass.

**Figure 4-1:** Tighten the arrowhead each time you pull it out from the target.

**Damage to your tackle**—Each time you nock the arrow and release it a number of things happen: the nock scrapes the bow string, the vanes brushes the side of the bow, the arrow's shaft slides over the arrow rest that is then hit by the vanes, the bow (arrow and string) gets subjected to tremendous sudden stress, the shooting glove gets scraped, and the target gets one more hole. The incoming arrow could also hit an already embedded one. Damage to your arrows may not be the same as the damage to my arrows if you use standard archery targets.

**Arrowheads**—Screwed in arrowheads might become loose when the arrow rotates counterclockwise on its way to the target. If the arrow rotates clockwise, it will tighten the arrowhead. Whichever way the arrow rotates, make it a practice to tighten the arrowhead after pulling it out of a target. Otherwise, you will eventually lose some.

**Arrow rests**—With a recurve bow, each time you shoot, the arrow slides over the arrow rest as it is propelled by the bow string. You will know when to replace the arrow rest. Its tip that supports the shaft will hang by a thread then will just drop of. The arrow rests I had lasted, on the average, 16,000 shots. The most recent one I had lasted 19,883 shots. From time to time, check that the arrow rest is tightly screwed or glued.

A compound bow's arrow rest completely encloses the shaft (Figure 3-6 above). While I improvised an arrow rest for my recurve, you can't do the same for a compound bow.

 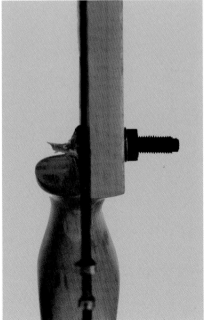

An arrow rest (Figure 4-2) could last as many as 19,000 shots. If you do not have a spare, you can make one from a discarded plastic vane by cutting it to the proper size and gluing it to the base. The improvised arrow rest (Figure 4-3) cradles the arrow in place and could last about 5,000 shots.

**Figure 4-2:** Arrow rest.    **Figure 4-3:** Improvised arrow rest.

**Figure 4-4**

**Figure 4-5**

**The bow**—When not in use, place the bow where it can't be stepped on, sat on, or exposed to excessive heat or cold. Unstring your recurve bow if you are to store it indefinitely. If you store a stringed bow, the string should not carry any load other than the stress it is subjected to by both ends of the bow.

⦿ **Recurve bow**—When I shoot and decide to take a break like making iced tea or hot coffee or do something in my computer, I place the bow on a chair in the shade of a tree to prevent it from warping. The bow is not supposed to warp and the arrows are not supposed to bend but I still go through the routine. (During these breaks sometimes robins use the bow as a perch.)

⦿ **Compound bow**—You can't lay down a compound bow on its side on a hard flat surface because of its irregular shape. For this purpose, I place the compound bow on its riser (on top of cardboard) between two blocks of wood to prevent it from toppling.

**Bow string**—Repeated nocking of arrows at the same spot will eventually fray the serving then the string breaks. You must check the serving from time to time to see if it is starting to fray. If it does, don't take the chance of it breaking during use. Replace it right away.

⦿ **Compound bow**—A compound bow can be re-strung by hand if you are an old hand at it. However, it is best to go to an authorized dealer who has the experience and the

I place the recurve flat on its side on a chair (Figure 4-4) or even on vines (Figure 4-5) when I retrieve my arrows. On the other hand, I have to very carefully place the compound bow on top of a cardboard (Figure 4-6) sandwiched by blocks of wood to prevent it from toppling.

**Figure 4-6**

bow press needed to replace the bowstring. A compound bowstring must be replaced with a new bowstring.

A compound bow is never unstrung. The bowstring must always be waxed.

◉ **Recurve bow**—The shortest lived bowstring I had lasted 17,315 shots; the longest, 36,621 shots. That is before I decided to improvise.

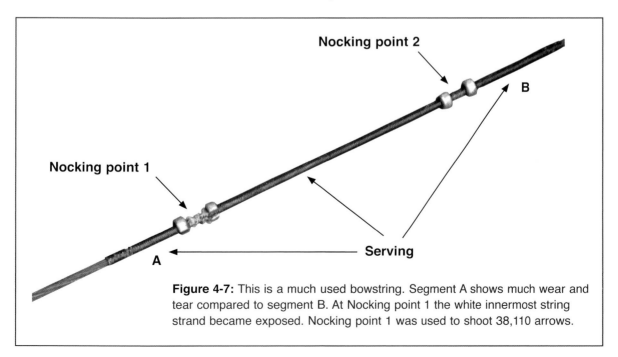

**Figure 4-7:** This is a much used bowstring. Segment A shows much wear and tear compared to segment B. At Nocking point 1 the white innermost string strand became exposed. Nocking point 1 was used to shoot 38,110 arrows.

The life of the recurve bowstring can be extended by switching the loops because the nocking point is not at the middle (See Figure 1-24 on page 31). In Figure 4-7, Nocking point 2 is practically a new bowstring with a new set of string nocks. This can easily extend the useful life of the bowstring by at least 50%. I tried to remove the original pair of string nocks but it was clamped tight. So I left it alone. Nocking point 2, so far, had launched 20,490 arrows. Hence, this particularly bow string had lasted about 58,000 shots.

**Figure 4-8:** At extreme left is an unused arrow. The other two have damaged nocks.

**Figure 4-9:** Arrows with damaged fletchings. At extreme right is one that got sheared by an incoming arrow.

Do not wait too long to switch the loops. As soon as the innermost white strand becomes exposed make the switch. In my case, I waited too long.

**Fletchings**—If your target is not thick enough, the arrow will penetrate all the way to the fletchings. The fletchings will start to tear (Figure 4-9, extreme left) and eventually shear. Fletchings can be sheared by incoming arrows (Figure 4-9, extreme right).

Fletchings (Figure 4-9, middle) can be glued back on by using school glue. Fletchings can be replaced but it will take some practice to do it properly.

**Nocks**—One might feel good when he had shot a good group. However, good grouping could result in a bad thing. For example: If you had become accurate in hitting a 6" circle, you could "Robin Hood" your arrow damaging the nock (Figure 4-8), the shaft, or the fletchings (Figure 4-9).

Nocks are available separately. Hence, damaged nocks can easily be replaced.

**Compound bow**—Replace damaged nocks with commercial nocks.

**Recurve bow**—If you do not want to miss your scheduled bow shoot, you can make nocks from small tree branches. Duplicate the dimensions of the plastic nocks. Use a Dremel or a saw to cut the groove. Use a carpet cutter to widen the groove then using a metallic nail file or folded sandpaper to smooth the groove to fit the serving.

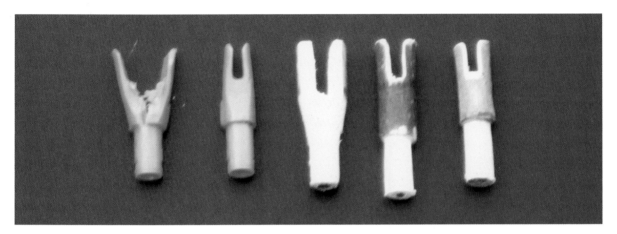

**Figure 4-10:** Left to right: a damaged plastic nock, an unused plastic nock, a nock made from rattan, two other wooden nocks made from tree branches. Notice that the grooves of the wooden nocks are wider than that of the plastic nock and hence can be used only with the split finger grip. While the inside of the grooves of the wooden nocks were smoothed with sandpaper, the seemingly smooth wood fibers could damage the serving.

The wooden nock, as it dries, will shrink and could slip out of the shaft. Hence, make more than you actually need. Do not throw away loose wooden nocks. Dip the part of the nock inserted into the shaft in water for a minute to make it swell. Without waiting for it to dry, insert it into the shaft. It will fit until it dries again. (At one time, out of curiosity, I put a nock that just fits into the shaft in a microwave for one minute. It dried and shrunk. I had to dip it in water to make it swell.)

The wooden nock will have different weights. In effect, each of your arrows will have different weights. I have shot 5 arrows with wooden nocks and 5 arrows with commercial plastic nocks. I have good shooting percentages with both sets. Remember though that wooden nocks are only for temporary use as it could split as you release the bow string. However, even plastic commercial nocks could break due to wear and tear.

**Shaft**—Damage to shafts can result from impacts of the arrow against hard objects. Shafts can also be damaged if pulled out from the target at the wrong angle. The arrow must be pulled out as close to the point of entry as possible and along the angle it is embedded.

Check for cracks along the length of the shaft by rotating it inside your palm along its length.

Arrows could crack at the point where the nock is seated on the shaft. This is mostly due to occasional Robin Hood shots. Sometimes the crack is not visible but you can feel it by rotating the shaft's end between your fingers. The nocks of these arrows will not have a tight fit. Discard shafts that have cracks.

**Shooting Glove**—The shooting glove will get scuffed after much use to the extent that it could prevent the smooth release of the string that will likely cause an errant shot. To extend its useful life dust it with talcum powder.

**Figure 4-11:** Duct tape around the index finger will prevent the glove from getting pulled as the arrow is released.

As the string is released, it could pull the scuffed glove out of the index finger. If this happens, put duct tape around the index finger glove. This will extend the useful life of the finger glove until you decide to buy a new one.

# PART II: Safety and Preparation

## CHAPTER 5

# SAFE SHOOTING

There is always the probability of getting injured when one engages in any physical activity. Even when you are shooting alone it's very possible to experience some pain or suffer some self-inflicted injury. Bows can fail. In fact, it is possible that a compound bow, with its many parts, could shatter. It's something you should be aware of, and prepared to deal with. However, the best way to avoid any possible injuries is to be safety conscious.

# Safety Guidelines

Archery may be a fun activity but never forget that a bow and the arrow that it propels is a potentially deadly weapon. Hence, you must take the strictest safety precautions to prevent injury to individuals or damage to property when you shoot.

Here is a worst-case scenario. Your house has a common wire fence with the neighbor to the right and with the neighbor to the left. There is a road with constant traffic just over the fence at the back. Hence, the *safest* direction you can shoot is *toward* your house. However, this poses a danger to your family as well as your property. Despite such a limited choice, you can minimize the risks by observing the following guidelines.

1.  In the beginning, shoot from a modest distance of 10 feet; after a few thousand shots from 20 feet, and so on up to the maximum safe distance you can shoot from.
2.  Keep children indoors and alert other family members that you will be shooting the bow.
3.  Young archers must be strictly supervised.
4.  Do not shoot if any of your neighbors are in their backyards.
5.  Use the lighter weight bow, say, one with a 32 lbs. pull as well as bullet-shaped arrowheads.
6.  Use a wide target.
7.  Locate your target far enough away from the house such that even if you do miss the "broad side of a barn" there is little likelihood that the arrow will break a glass window or put a hole on the siding.
8.  The target must be of such material that the arrow will get embedded in and not pass through it.
9.  Do not do any snap shooting.
10. Do not allow a friend/guest to shoot a bow in your backyard.

You should also minimize the possibility of injury to your person by
1.  Wearing safety goggles.
2.  Inspecting the bow and arrow (shaft, nock) for cracks, dents, and other damage marks.
3.  Inspecting the bowstring for signs of fraying of the serving.

If you will be shooting in your yard, it is important that you check your local ordinances.

# Avoiding Distractions

You need only a few seconds to focus on your target. However, as short as it seems, one can get distracted by a number of things. Some you can control. Others you can't.

Distractions can be physical or mental.

## Physical Distractions

- Bugs/insects/mosquitoes could be dancing in front of your eyes. As you shoot, you might get a glimpse of a mosquito feasting on your arm. It is easy enough to accidentally inhale a gnat.
- If there are trees where you shoot, there will be birds. Occasionally, a bird could fly between you and the target.
- Heat and cold could make you uncomfortable that could make you release the arrow prematurely. You will tend to hurry up your shots.
- Wind causing leaves to sway could distract you. Strong enough a crosswind could push your arrow away from the target.
- If you shoot at dusk or early in the morning there might not be enough light.

## Defective eyesight will not help you hit the target

- Fatigue could cause you to release the arrow prematurely.
- If you are over bowed, you will be struggling to get to your anchor point.
- You might catch a glimpse of the an individual appearing in your peripheral vision.

## Mental Distractions

- If you already hit the target 4 times and you still have to shoot a fifth arrow, doubt could cross your mind
- Target size/shape could become mental clutter (See Figure 8-1).
- Concern about damaging already-embedded arrows will make you think too much and will affect your aim.
- Mental clutter such as unpaid bills or a parking ticket could cross your mind as you shoot.
- Mental clutter such as concern of hitting the house's siding.

Nobody is immune to mental clutter. However, total focus can be achieved. No. I don't empty my mind. I fill my mind with only one thought one image—the target. In this moment, the outside world doesn't exist.

You can minimize physical distractions. For example: Avoid shooting the bow when mosquitoes or gnats are active. To avoid the heat, shoot early in the morning. To fend off cold, dress accordingly. Don't shoot when the weather forecasts 25 mph wind. You can shoot when you are fatigued but do not hurry up your shots. You can wear corrective eye glasses.

I used to do long pole forms under a big tree that has a low overhanging branch. One of the movements in the form required a 360 degree turn that was simultaneous with a sweep with the long pole. At the 180 degree portion of the turn, I felt a jar on my long pole. I stopped and looked up. The branch was too high up and a robin had flown into my pole and was killed. You can not prevent birds from flying where they want to. I felt horrible!

CHAPTER 6

# AVOIDING INJURIES

In shooting the bow, the bow hand, the string hand, and the back muscles are subjected to a lot of stress. Hence, your chances of suffering injury would increase if you are over bowed. As a martial artist, I have suffered many injuries over the years: I have broken my left hand; I have developed stick fighting's equivalent of tennis elbow; I have suffered numerous bruises and generally experienced a lot of pain. In archery, while I have not experienced any problems with my wrist, I have suffered an elbow injury. Calluses (see Figure 6-1) are always a possibility; however, it is not likely that you will get calluses in your bow hand when you shoot the compound bow. Its grip is more archer-friendly.

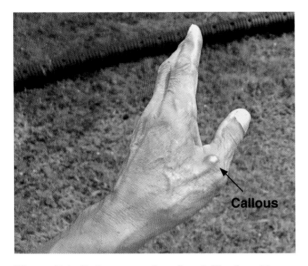

**Figure 6-1:** Callus on my bow hand. The knuckle of my bow thumb looks abnormal. It is calloused as it supports the recurve bow when I shoot. Depending on the size of your hands, you might or might not get calloused. I use a nail file to reduce the thickness of the callus.

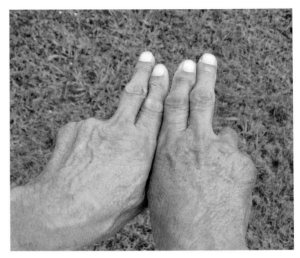

**Figure 6-2:** My string fingers (right) are bigger than my bow fingers (left). The sun rises on my right hand side. Hence, my right hand is darker than my left hand.

One of my students took a job in another state and didn't visit for over a year. On the first day he came back, he asked, "Are your fingers broken?" I said, "No." He was looking at my string fingers. From his angle, it must have looked bad. My index and middle fingers are bent a few degrees more to the right than normal and are bigger than my bow fingers (see Figure 6-2). No wonder he thought they were broken.

The degree of discomfort you will experience will depend on your goal. A goal of shooting 100 arrows a day is reasonable. It will take about 40 minutes to do so. A goal of shooting 100,000 arrows in one year is not practical. If you do, you may rush and ignore safety precautions. This could lead to harmful consequences. A more realistic goal would be to shoot 50 **quality** shots a day—shots properly aimed and released with the mind totally focused.

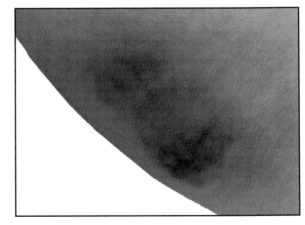

**Figure 6-3:** A bruise could result if you shoot without a forearm guard. (Courtesy Thoraya Zedan)

Shooting the bow is relatively safe. However, if you run, jump, or do some other stunts while shooting, the likelihood of suffering injury increases many fold. If you shoot your bow with safety in mind and with good common sense as a guide, your chances of suffering pain or injury can be substantially reduced.

# Warming Up

One of the best ways to avoid injuring yourself, along with following safety guidelines, is to prepare your muscles for shooting before every outing. Shooting the bow uses mainly the neck, arm, and back muscles. These are subjected to stresses each time you pull the bow string. Hence, it is good practice to exercise them before you shoot.

**Neck**—Whether you use the open or close stance, your head will be turned toward your target. This means that your head is turned to one side when shooting. To exercise the other side of the neck, with hands on hips

- Look to your left then to your right
- Look up then look down
- Tilt your head to the right then to the left
- Rotate your head with your chin touching your chest, shoulder, and with the back of your head touching your back

Do at least five repetitions slowly.

**Arms**—You should loosen up your arms.
- Rotate your arms at the front one way then rotate them the opposite way
- Rotate your arms at your side clockwise then counterclockwise

Do at least five repetitions slowly.

**Shoulders**—Rotate your shoulders clockwise then counterclockwise. Do at least five repetitions slowly.

I made a bow from ½" PVC pipe (Figures 6-4 and 6-5) and used it to duplicate the drawing of a bow. It takes about a 10-15 lb pull, which is a lot less than the weight of the bow that an adult archer would use. However, it would be good to stretch the same muscles that you would use in drawing your bow.

**FIGURE 6-4**                    **FIGURE 6-5**

The bow pictured here (Figures 6-4 and 6-5) is not designed to be shot but is used to warm up muscles that are stressed when a bow is drawn. The drawing of a bow can be duplicated by use of exercise bands. It took about 20 minutes to make this one.

Hold the bow then slowly draw the string right handed. At the end of the draw, hold still for about 15 seconds or longer. Repeat drawing the string left handed. There are commercially available devices that duplicate the drawing of a bow that you could also use when you warm up.

Figures 6-6 and 6-7 show an isometric exercise. Hold your hands as shown. Simultaneously, push with your front hand and pull with the other. Hold for about 10 seconds. Repeat changing the roles of the left and the right hands.

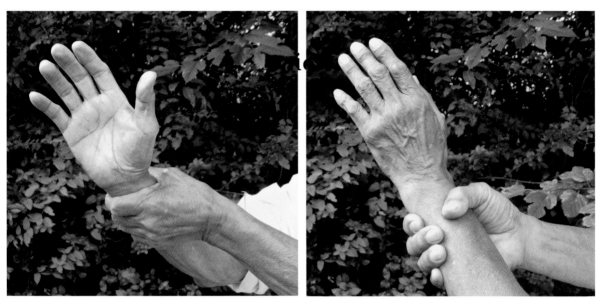

**Figure 6-6:** Pull with your left and push with your right.

**Figure 6-7:** Push your left and pull with your right.

A similar exercise can be done using a living tree branch (Figures 6-8 and 6-9). Assume either the close or open stance. Grasp the branch with your left hand, push then hold for about 10 seconds. In turn, grasp the branch with your right hand, pull then hold for about 10 seconds.

**Figure 6-8:** Push with your left hand.

**Figure 6-9:** Pull with your right hand.

If you consistently exercise and warm up before shooting it will become second nature. And if you combine a warming up routine with the safe shooting practices outlined in Chapter 5 you will stand a much better chance of avoiding injuries.

# PART III: Technique and Progress

CHAPTER 7

# SHOOTING THE BOW

Learning to shoot a bow is a process that includes preparation, planning and execution. In order to effectively shoot, you should take into account a number of factors that affect your performance. These include everything from making sure your tackle is in good working condition to understanding the mechanics of shooting.

Your tackle must be in good working condition if you are to shoot tight groups or achieve high scores. Hence, before you shoot check:

- The bow and the arrows for cracks.
- If the serving at the nocking point is not frayed.
- That the index fletching is perpendicular to the bowstring and with its edge skyward when the arrow is nocked (Figure 7-1).
- That your target is properly set up.
- That other persons present when you shoot are to your back and several feet away from you.

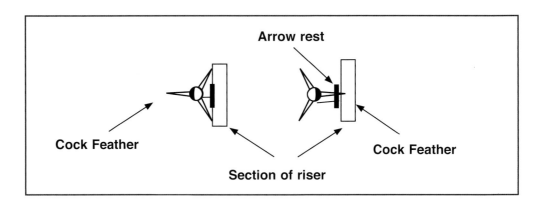

**Figure 7-1:** Properly nocked, the two other vanes will glide over the side of center cut (left). Improperly nocked, the index fletching will hit the side of center cut (right). There will be no such concern when shooting the compound bow. (Not to scale.)

## Shooting Distance

Recreational shooting can be done in a backyard where space is limited. It will be smart and safe to start shooting your bow from 10 feet. Stay at this distance until you have taken 1,000 arrow shots. Next, shoot from 15 feet with the same number of arrows. Then shoot from 30 feet (10 yards) shooting the same number of arrows. Increase your shooting distance to 20 yards. Shoot from the maximum safe distance only when you feel confident that you can control your shots.

Archery is very popular around the world and is an Olympic sport. In the Olympics only recurve bows are used. Listed below are the shooting distances and the sizes of the targets used in the Olympics and in indoor competitions.

| Event | Distance (m.) | Target diameter (cm.) |
| --- | --- | --- |
| Indoors | 18 or 25 | 40 (outermost circle) |
| Olympics | 70 or 90 | 122 (outermost circle) |

**Table 7-1.** Competition distances (metric system)

| Event | Distance (yd.) | Target diameter (in.) |
| --- | --- | --- |
| Indoors | 20 or 27* | 16* |
| Olympics | 76 or 98* | 48* |

**Table 7-2.** Competition distances (converted to the English system) *Rounded numbers

| In this work | Distance (yd.) | Target dimensions (in.) |
| --- | --- | --- |
| Backyard | 20 or 25 | 8, 6, 4, 2 circles |
| Backyard | 20 or 25 | Upper body (Figure 7-31) |

**Table 7-3.** Distances used in this book (English system)

# Mechanics of Shooting the Bow

The mechanics of shooting a recurve bow is not any different from that of shooting a compound bow. Shooting the bow consists of stance, nocking the arrow, drawing the string, aiming the point, releasing the arrow, and following through. I will call this sequence as shooting mechanics.

You must have good shooting mechanics if you are to consistently hit your target. You will not be consistent if you have to struggle to bring your string hand to your anchor point. When you shoot, your focus must be on the target. The draw must happen without any thought given to it. This will not be possible if you are over bowed. It takes me about 40 minutes to shoot 100 arrows, in sets of five, from a distance of 20 yards. This time includes the 20 round trips I needed to retrieve the arrows from the target. I pause for several seconds between shots to give my arm and back muscles time to return to a relaxed state.

In the process of shooting, you will develop a certain rhythm between getting the arrow from the quiver and releasing it. It takes me about 10 to 12 seconds to take the arrow from the quiver, to nock the arrow, and to release the arrow. Releasing the arrow too quickly is called snap shooting—which is not good. Filming your shots will help determine whether you are releasing the arrow too fast, too slow, or just right.

Shooting the bow requires good form. Table 7-4 compares the mechanics of shooting the bow, shooting the slingshot, and throwing a knife.

| Shooting the bow | Shooting the slingshot | Throwing a knife |
| --- | --- | --- |
| 1. Stance | 1. Stance | 1. Stance |
| 2. Nocking the arrow | 2. Loading the projectile | 2. Gripping the knife |
| 3. Simultaneously pushing the bow and pulling the string | 3. Simultaneously pushing the "Y" and pulling the rubber band | 3. Pull back of throwing arm |
| 4. Momentary stop when anchor is reached | 4. Momentary stop at maximum pull | 4. Momentary stop at the end of the pull back |
| 5. Aiming using the arrowhead as guide | 5. Aiming using the "Y" as guide | 5. Aiming is not done physically but with the eye and the brain |
| — | — | 6. Swing forward |
| 6. Release | 6. Release | 7. Release |
| 7. Follow through | 7. Follow through | 8. Follow through |

**Table 7-4.** Mechanics of shooting the bow, using the sling shot, and throwing a knife.

You might ask, "What does shooting the slingshot or throwing the knife have to do with shooting the bow?" One similarity is obvious: all involve the use of stored energy to propel a projectile. However, the one critical similarity is, all three involve releasing a projectile by relaxing the fingers. The ability to relax the fingers without conscious thought can mean the difference between a good shot and a bad shot.

**Figure 7-2:** Closed stance.          **Figure 7-3:** Open stance.

In the closed stance (Figure 7-2) the feet are parallel; in the open stance (Figure 7-3), left foot is slightly turned.

**Stance**—Stand with the side of the body nearly perpendicular to the target. Weight must be equally carried by both feet and posture is relaxed. The feet can be positioned in two ways: in the close stance or in the open stance. I prefer the open stance (Figure 7-3).

**Nock the arrow**—Rotate the arrow to nock it between the string nocks such that the index fletching is skyward (Figure 7-4).

FIGURE 7-4          FIGURE 7-5

**Figure 7-4 to 7-9** Close ups of nocking the arrow and the grip on the bow string. With some types of arrow rests (see Figure 3-5 above), it is not necessary to put the index finger on the shaft.

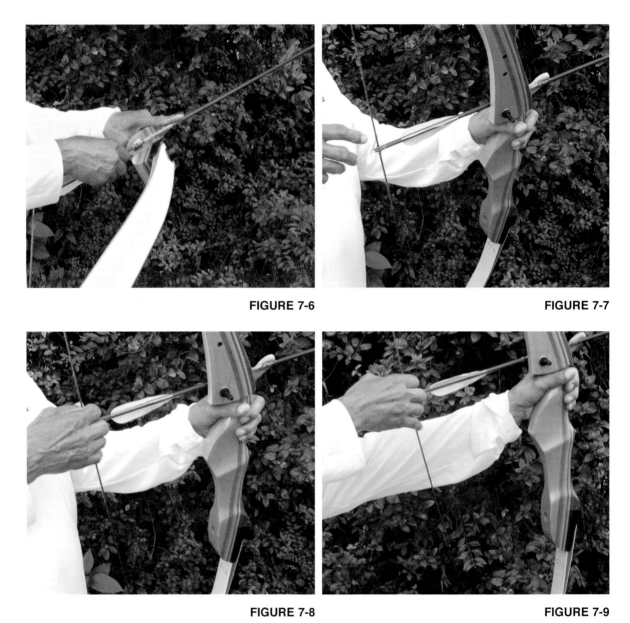

FIGURE 7-6                                    FIGURE 7-7

FIGURE 7-8                                    FIGURE 7-9

Lay the arrow on the arrow rest (Figure 7-5) then place your index finger on the shaft (Figure 7-6). Rotate the bow so that it forms a small angle with your body (Figure 7-7). For the right-handed shooter, the upper limb will tilt slightly to the right. This tilt will help prevent the arrow from sliding off the arrow rest. Place your string arm on the string putting the arrow between your index and middle fingers (Figure 7-8).

Raise the bow to point the arrowhead about 30° skyward (Figure 7-9).

**Draw**—Simultaneously, lower the arrowhead, pull the string, and push the bow slowly, smoothly, and continuously. Remove your index finger at a time that you are most comfortable. If you hesitate and double pull, you will likely miss the target (Figure 7-17, Figure 7-18). Continue the draw until you reach your anchor point (Figure 7-19).

**Aim**—Aim by moving your bow arm. Use the tip of the arrow and the center of the target as the guide to your aim. In my case, I had the tendency to shoot to the left. I made adjustments (Figure 7-10).

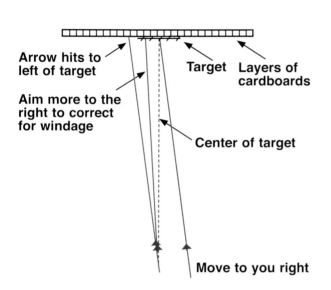

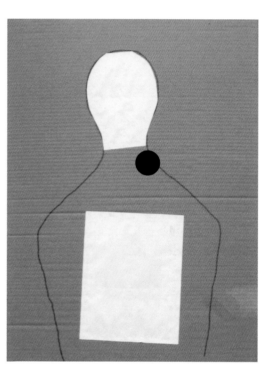

Figure 7-10: If your first shot hits to the left of the target, to correct your aim, you can move to your right, or you can aim the point the arrowhead more to the right, or you can do both.

Figure 7-11: Aiming configuration— The dot represents the tip of the arrowhead. Target is the head.

In the beginning, I aimed consciously, moving the arrowhead to point at the target (Figure 7-19). After several thousand shots, a picture got imprinted in my brain. This picture is shown in Figure 7-11 which shows the position of the arrowhead (black dot) in relation to the target. When I see this configuration, I release the arrow.

There is more than one black dot when I aim at the rectangular piece and even more when I aim to hit the whole of the upper body. The elevation of the dot will depend on the archer's distance from the target. After thousands of shot, you will aim by feel and will see nothing but the spot you aim to hit.

Shoot with both eyes open.

**Figure 7-12:** Open stance.

**Figure 7-13A:** Take arrow from the quiver.

**Figure 7-13B:** Pull the arrow out gently.

**Figure 7-14:** Nock the arrow.

**Figure 7-15:** Lay the arrow on the arrow rest.

**Figure 7-16:** Pull the string slightly and place the left index finger on the shaft.

**Figure 7-17A:** Rotate the bow then grip the arrow between the index and middle fingers.

**Figure 7-17B:** Point the arrowhead skyward (about 30°) then slowly bring it down as you draw.

**Figure 7-18:** Continue the draw.

**Figure 7-19:** Remove the index finger from the arrow and bring it beside the middle finger to help in the grip as you draw to the anchor point.
If you have to, aim by moving your bow hand.

**Figure 7-20:** Relax your string fingers to release the arrow.

**Figure 7-21:** Follow through.

**Figure 7-22:** High anchor – The string does not touch the face. The knuckle of the thumb is pressed against the hollow of the cheek.

**Figure 7-23:** Low anchor – The string touches the tip of the nose and the upper lip. The "V" formed by the thumb and index finger is pressed against the jaw.

**Release**—Relax your fingers to allow the bowstring to slide off the shooting glove (Figure 7-20). At the time of release, no thought is given to the action of the fingers. The mind is focused on the target.

Here, the condition of the shooting glove is critical. If it is scuffed, there will be a tiny bump in it that will affect the smooth release of the arrow. If you release the arrow before taking the time to aim, that is snap shooting and very likely your shot will go wild.

**Follow through**—This does not require motion. You must remain in the release position until you hear the sound of or see the arrow hitting the target (Figure 7-21).

The high or the low anchor completes the draw. I use the high anchor.

# Developing Good Form

If you have not handled a bow before, you would like to shoot your first arrow right away and most likely, hurriedly. However, that is not the way to developing good form. Slowly is the best way. Stand about 10 feet from your target. Go slowly through the sequence illustrated above in Figures 7-4 through 7-9. After feeling comfortable with this, go through the sequence in Figure 7-12 through Figure 7-21.

After a thousand shots, shoot from 15 feet. Take another thousand shots from 20 feet and so on. Proceeding slowly is better than hurrying up the learning process. Taking time to learn slowly is the quickest way to developing good form.

**Figure 7-24:** The nock is between the index and middle fingers. This called the split finger grip.

**Figure 7-25:** The nock is above the index finger. Two of the grips used on the bowstring.

The process of shooting the compound bow is really no different from shooting the recurve. The shooting mechanics developed in shooting one will carry over to shooting the other. The main difference in shooting the two bows will be felt in the draw. Otherwise, the process is the same.

Figures 7-2 to 7-21 explain the physical aspects of placing and nocking the arrow, drawing the bowstring, aiming, releasing the arrow, and the follow up. The same actions are shown in Figures 7-26A to 7-26N. This is a good time to explain why archery is very much a physical activity as it is a cerebral one.

As you take the arrow from the quiver (Figures 7-26A to 7-26C) you should begin thinking about the aiming process. The length of time you spend on looking at the target imprints an image in your brain. Simultaneously, you should fill your mind with one thought, one image—the target.

**Figure 7-26A:** Shooting a compound bow.

**Figure 7-26B**

**Figure 7-26C**

**Figure 7-26D**

Figure 7-26E

Figure 7-26F

Figure 7-26G

Figure 7-26H

In Figure 7-26D, the archer takes his eye off the target for a few split seconds. He does not lose the image in his brain. It stays there until he looks at the target again (Figure 7-26E) where he resumes the aiming process. He is totally focused—as he achieves full draw (Figure 7-26M).

The release of the arrow is an explosion of the stored energy in the bow. At the time of release, the string hand is completely relaxed and as before, the mind is filled only with one thought—the target.

Figure 7-26I

Figure 7-26J

FIGURE 7-26K

FIGURE 7-26L

FIGURE 7-26M

FIGURE 7-26N

# The Target

I throw knives, shoot the blowgun, and shoot the bow. Logic dictates that I should have three different targets. However, three targets will clutter a 70" by 100" backyard. Hence, I designed one set up that is suitable for all three. I use two target supports: one fixed; the other, movable. I shoot at the fixed target from 20 yards; at the movable target from 25 yards. The latter is the maximum safe distance from which I can shoot the bow.

**Target support**—The target support is made of two 4"×4"×4" posts (cut from an 8" long timber) buried 1" deep. Nailed to the posts on opposite sides is a pair of 1"×4" planks that form something like a tuning fork. The 4" gap between each pair of planks can easily accommodate 5 layers of cardboard. The total height of the target support from the ground is about 6 feet. The cardboards are placed on top of the plank that straddles the tuning forks.

I have no pole digger. I used a throwing ax to start the hole then a long pointed all-metal throwing dagger to dig the 12" deep hole. I used a garden scoop and a sardine can to remove the dirt. After placing the 4"×4"×4" posts in the hole. I filled the gaps with the dirt and tamped it down with a short 2"×4". The target support costs about $35 including a box of nails.

**Figure 7-27:** Target front view—The posts are 36" (center to center) apart.

**Figure 7-28:** Target side view—The target support looks like a tuning fork viewed from the side.

**Figure 7-29:** A rectangular frame is inserted on which cardboards will be clamped.

This is not the location of my target but merely shows details of the support against an uncluttered background.

**Target**—My target consists of several layers of cardboard. On the top cardboard are glued my targets. The concentric circles (Figure 7-33) are designed to help develop instinctive shooting since you have to change your aim four times. In addition, this set up will prevent damage to arrows by shooting only one arrow at each circle. Clamps minimize movement of the cardboards. One third of a 4 fluid oz. bottle of glue is sufficient for use on paper targets that lasted about 25,000 shots.

Most of my life, I have trained in the martial arts and any activity I engage in is geared toward self defense. Hence, one of my other targets is the upper body (Figures 7-30 and

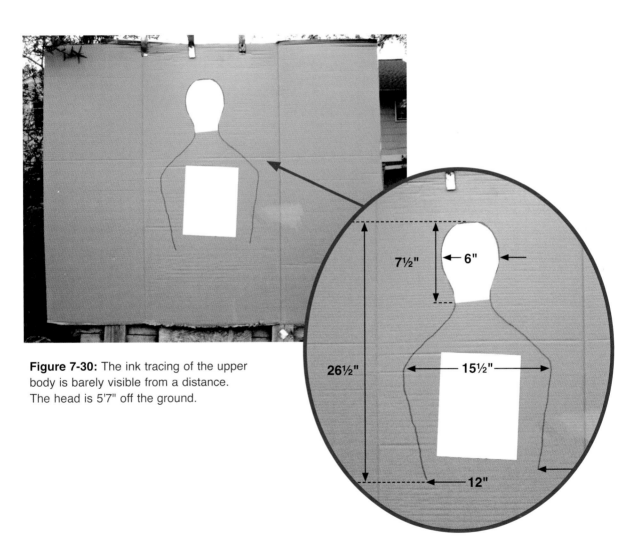

**Figure 7-30:** The ink tracing of the upper body is barely visible from a distance. The head is 5'7" off the ground.

**Figure 7-31:** Dimensions of the upper body. The cardboards are clamped to reduce movement. A plastic tarp protects the cardboards from rain and snow.

7-31). This target is shooter-friendly. If you aim at the head or the rectangular piece and miss, you can still hit something—the rest of the upper body.

You can get the outline of the upper body that is used as targets for shooting guns. Trace it on a cardboard then cut it out. This will serve as your pattern. Whenever you need a new target, place the cut out on a cardboard then trace it. The glued shapes on the tracing make the target more visible. I use paper I get from junk mail. Cardboard does not cost anything and is easy to replace after it becomes mutilated. You can get it from your neighborhood grocery store. They will only be too happy to give them away.

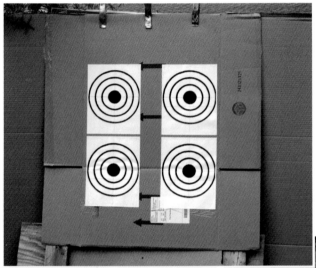

**Figure 7-32:** Targets with concentric circles mounted above the ground.

**Figure 7-33:** A target support can be a simple rectangular frame set on the ground and leaning against a pair of posts. This set up is recommended for beginners.

CHAPTER 8

# INSTINCTIVE SHOOTING

Instinctive shooting does not mean that the archer is not aiming—although it will look like so. It merely means that there is no sight attached to his bow. In the beginning, you will consciously aim using the tip of the arrow and the target as guide. Eventually after thousands of shots a particular configuration that your arrow forms with the target will become imprinted in your brain. The instant, you see this particular configuration— much like a picture—is the cue to release the arrow.

Take a look at Figure 8-1. The targets have different sizes... but not really. From the standpoint of the archer, he would be aiming at the smallest circle (at left) which is the same size as the black circle (right). However, if the archer misses the innermost 2-inch circle, he will still score. On the other hand, if he misses the 2" circle (at right), he scores 0. Mental clutter could make you miss.

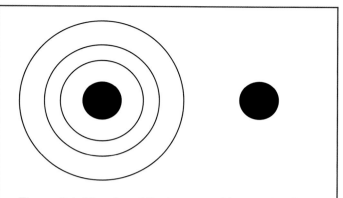

**Figure 8-1:** The size of the target could mentally affect the bowman. At left, a 2" circle is inside three bigger circles. At right, the 2" circle stands alone.

I normally shoot at multiple targets with 5 arrows. I do not number the targets. As I get an arrow from the quiver, I decide which target to aim at. After the first shot, I choose the target at random. One time, a student watched me shoot. As I released the arrow, she exclaimed, "You are not aiming!" But I was.

**Figure 8-2:** Targets of different sizes and arrangements will test your aim and could become a distraction.

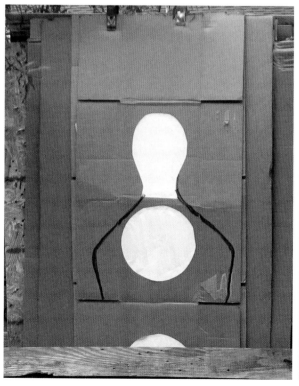

**FIGURE 8-2A:** 8" circle and upper body.

**FIGURE 8-2B:** Two 8" circles and upper body.

**FIGURE 8-2C** Two 8" circles.

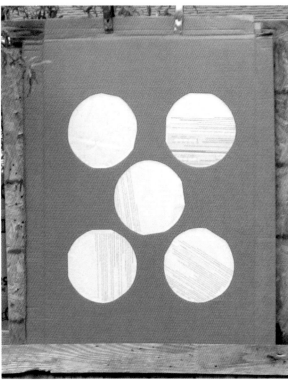

**FIGURE 8-2D:** Five 8" circles.

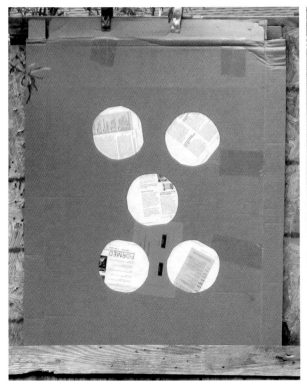

**FIGURE 8-2E :** Five 6" circles.

**FIGURE 8-2F:** Concentric circles with 8", 6", 4", 2" diameters.

Aiming is not a single movement. Rather, it is a series of movements that ends with the arrow being pointed toward the target. Aiming starts mentally. At the time I take an arrow from the quiver, I decide which target to shoot at. As I nock the arrow, I could have a change of mind and aim at another target. I don't. If I do, it is very likely that I will miss the target.

The series of aiming movements (Figure 8-3) starts with nocking the arrow (A, B) raising the arrowhead and pointing it skyward (C, D), then slowly lowering (E) it to point at the target.

At the time I feel that the arrowhead is at the right elevation and is in a proper left/right placement, I hold the position and then I immediately release the arrow. My eyes and my mind guide the arrow. You can say I will the arrow into the target. If you are interested in instinctive shooting, you should practice this process on a daily basis until it becomes second nature.

**FIGURE 8-3A, (above left)** and **FIGURE 8-3B (above right):** Aiming is a series of movements.

**FIGURE 8-3C:** Start raising the bow skyward.

**FIGURE 8-3D:** Peak of skyward motion.

**FIGURE 8-3E:** Lower bow and right/left placement.

**FIGURE 8-3F:** Release and follow through.

**Figure 8-4:** A target consisting of plastic bottles of three sizes. For better visibility, the bottles were sprayed with fluorescent orange paint. The bottles could be filled with marbles to prevent movement when the wind blows. (I got this wooden frame from a neighbor who was only too happy to give it away.)

CHAPTER 9

# ADVANCED INSTINCTIVE SHOOTING

Even if you have limited space, you can add variety to your shooting. You can shoot from different distances, at multiple targets, or against the norm. One other variant I practice is shooting at dusk when I could hardly see the target. In this instance, you cannot make corrections on your aim because you wouldn't see where the previous arrow hit. However, if you use glow-in-the dark nocks, you will have a point of reference for the next arrow. I have also shot my bow under full moon.

# Shooting from Different Distances

You can take 5 steps to your left or right and then shoot. Although there will be little change in your shooting distance, you will have to adjust your aim. In my case, during the hot months, I move from my normal shooting spot to shaded spots to my right which is closer and to my left which is farther from the target.

If you are shooting from 25 yards, you can advance to the 15-yard or 20-yard distance and then shoot. You will have to change the elevation of your shots when you shoot from different distances.

# Shooting at Multiple Targets

In the beginning, shoot at only one target. For example: Set up a target with only one concentric circle. When you are consistently able to put your arrows inside the circle set up one that has multiple targets (Figures 9-1 and 9-2).

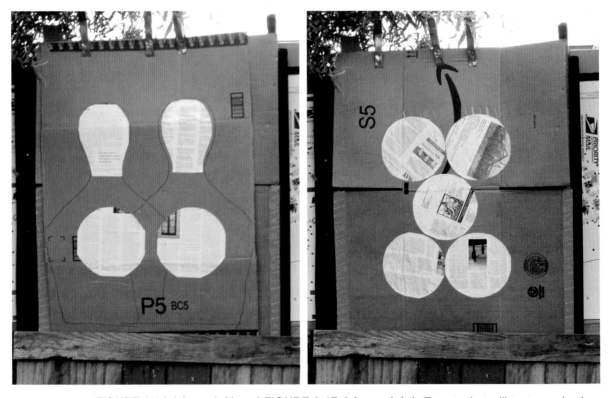

**FIGURE 9-1A (above left) and FIGURE 9-1B (above right):** Targets that will test your instinctive shooting. In A, you will have to change your aim four times; in B (8" circles), five times.

**FIGURE 9-2A:** Four 8" circles and a 4" circle at center.

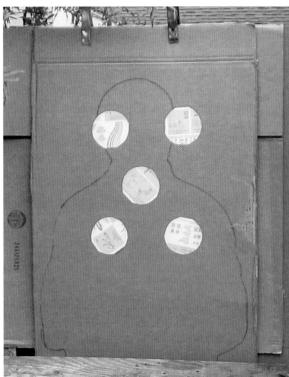

**FIGURE 9-2B:** Five 4" circles.

**Figure 9-2A to Figure 9-2C:** Originally, I planned to print my targets off the computer. However, I need a lot and printer ink is expensive. Hence, I cut out my targets from whatever paper becomes available. One time, I created a target using scrap paper without thinking of where it came from. I shot at the target and went to retrieve the arrows with one of my students. As we approached the target, she exclaimed, "Po, you are shooting at Mother Theresa! She is a saint!" Sure enough, the paper had an image of Mother Theresa. I changed the target. (My students call me Po which is short for Apo meaning grandfather in Tagalog.)

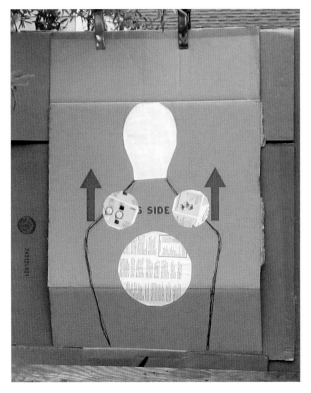

**FIGURE 9-2C:** Upper body with one 8" and two 4" circles.

# Shooting against the Norm

These should only be done with the recurve bow—not with the compound bow.

Good arrows fly straight. What happens if you shoot defective arrows or arrows of different lengths?

**Shooting arrows of different lengths**—It is standard practice to shoot arrows of uniform weights. However, there is skill to be gained in shooting arrows of different weights (lengths): A shorter lighter arrow will have a flatter trajectory than a heavier longer arrow. Hence, you will have to change the elevation of your shots.

Figure 9-3 (A and B) shows two sets of seven (five 32" and two 29") arrows embedded on a target. In both instances, five were good shots, one near miss, and one missed shot. The 2-vaned arrows were near misses. Head sizes are 6" across. Shooting distance is 20 yards.

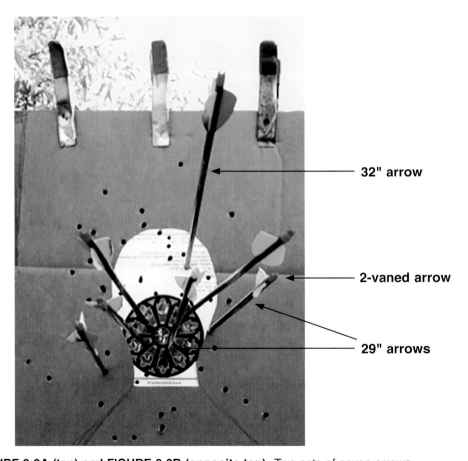

32" arrow

2-vaned arrow

29" arrows

**FIGURE 9-3A (top) and FIGURE 9-3B (opposite top):** Two sets of seven arrows.

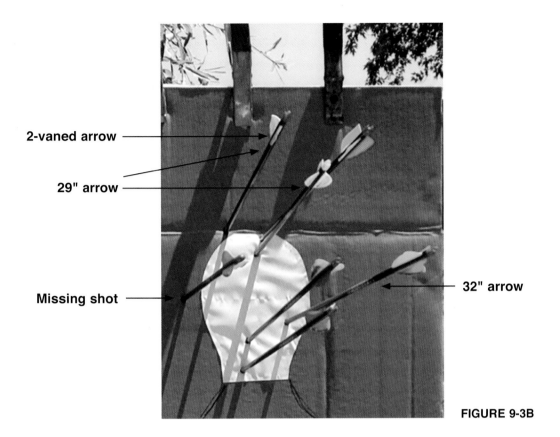

2-vaned arrow

29" arrow

Missing shot

32" arrow

**FIGURE 9-3B**

**Shooting arrows with 2 vanes versus 3 vanes**—After thousands of shots, many of my arrows got damaged. So I ended up having arrows with only one or two good vanes. Rather than throw them away, I removed the damaged fletchings and saved them. Remember the old adage? As soon as you throw something away, you'll need it the next day. Well, I needed it the next day! The day before I shot the 2-vaned and 3-vaned arrows, the fin-shaped part of the arrow rest got sheared. I did not have a spare. So I improvised by cutting a small piece of a discarded vane and attached it to the body of the arrow rest with glue used for vinyl repair. Surprisingly it worked. I shot these arrows with the improvised arrow rest (Figure 4-3). Later, I found that school glue worked just as well.

| Shooting distance is 20 yards | Hit | Miss | Total |
|---|---|---|---|
| 2 Vanes | 36 | 14 | 50 |
| 3 Vanes | 43 | 7 | 50 |
| Total | 79 | 21 | 100 |

**Table 9-1:** My scores shooting, in random order in sets of four, two 2-vaned and two 3-vaned arrows. The target is an 8" circle.

**Shooting an improperly nocked arrow**—When the lighter arrow is nocked with the index fletching in its proper orientation, the arrow flies straight.

On purpose, I nocked a few arrows with the index fletching oriented the other way. The lighter arrow fish-tailed—veered one way and then another as it flew toward the target. On the other hand, nocked the wrong way, the heavier arrow veered toward only one direction.

The unpredictability of the flight of an improperly nocked arrow is common knowledge. However, there is no harm in shooting a few improperly nocked arrows to see their behavior in flight.

**Shooting arrows with no vane and arrows with one vane**—I aimed arrows with no vane and one vane at the upper body—a big target that would allow for some erratic flights. They are both difficult shots. The trajectory of a no-vane or a one-vane arrow is unpredictable.

Figure 9-4 shows the vanes of the arrows I shoot. They have wooden nocks of different weights and have 1½ (an approximation), 2, or 3 vanes. They shoot equally well when properly nocked. When one of my students gave a questioning look at my arrows, I said, "If I miss what I am shooting at, I can blame it on my defective arrows. If I hit what I am shooting at, I can give myself a pat on the back!"

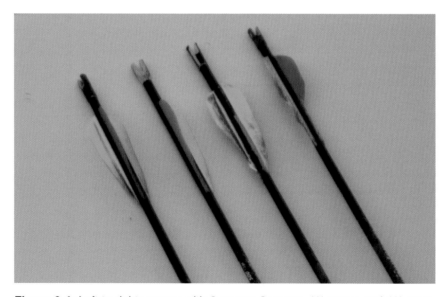

**Figure 9-4:** Left to right: arrows with 3 vanes; 2 vanes; 1½ vane; and 1½ vane.

CHAPTER 10

# ARROW SPEED AND TRAJECTORY

## Speed of the Arrow

I had always wondered how fast I throw a knife. At the time my book *The Art of Throwing* was published I had thrown knives/ax/shuriken/etc. 1.3 million times. However, I didn't know how fast I can throw a knife. That was kind of embarrassing although no one called my attention to it.

In 2016, Christmas came early for me. In July, a student gave me a speed detector. Finally I came to learn that I can throw a knife at about 52 mph which was the speed with which most serious knife throwers throw. However, I was most interested to see how fast an arrow travels.

So, I set up the speed detector on the ground directly in line with the path of the arrow and about 6½ feet away from the target as recommended in the instruction sheet that came with it. I shot a few arrows aiming at a target about 5'7" off the ground. The speed detector didn't flicker and gave no indication that it detected any motion. Obviously, there was something wrong with the set up. I used another target (Figure 10-1).

**Figure 10-1:** The speed detector is placed in line with the path of the arrow. I aimed just above the horizontal wood bar at the base of the frame. The two readings I took were taken at different times and temperatures: A, during summer (78˚F); B, in winter (8˚F). Due to the publisher's deadline, I had to shoot during winter.

The set up in the instruction sheet was for measuring the speed of a baseball pitch that is aimed at the strike zone which is between the top of the pants and the hollow beneath the knee cap. So I changed the elevation of my shot. I aimed even lower. In one of the shots, I nicked the 6" tall speed detector.

| | |
|---|---|
| **Shooting distance** | 20 yds. |
| **Bow** | Recurve |
| **Bow weight** | 32 lbs. |
| **Arrow material** | Carbon |
| **Arrow weight** | 286 grains (about 18 grams) |
| **Arrow length** | 32" |
| **Spine** | 500 |
| **Straightness** | .006 |
| **Temperature** | 78°F |
| **Speed detector*** | SmartPro Net Playz |

**Table 10-1** Specifics in the determination of arrow speed.

*The instruction sheet warned that the speed detector could give false readings when the humidity is high.

The variation in speed (106-126 ft./sec.) of the arrow shooting with the recurve can be attributed to the non-uniform weights of the arrows and slight differences in draw length. For example: If the draw length for the first shot is 27" and that of the next shot is 26¾" the speeds recorded will be different. If I used a clicker, the range of speed will be narrower.

Some of the 32" arrows I shot using the recurve have wooden nocks and heavier. The 32" arrows I used in shooting the compound bow were new and have uniform weights.

The speed of the 32" arrows ranged from 72 to 86 mph (106 ft./sec. to 126 ft./sec.) for the recurve; for the compound bow, maximum speed was 144 ft./sec. (Table 10-2). The speeds are within an order of magnitude of each other as to be expected. If you pull with a 32-lbs. draw weight on the bowstring of a recurve, you are going to get the about the same result as when you pull with the same 32-lbs. draw weight on the bowstring of a compound bow.

The difference in speeds of the arrows shot from the two bows could also be attributed to another factor. My compound bow is not much used whereas I have shot my recurve more than 200,000 times. My recurve bowstring has already launched 60,000 arrows. Hence, my 32 lbs. recurve could very well be pulling only 30 lbs.

I shoot 28" and 32" arrows with my compound bow. The range of speeds for 28" arrows was 164 kph—174 kph (149 ft./sec.—153 ft./sec.). The lighter 28" arrow traveled faster than the heavier 32" arrow as expected.

| Arrow length, inch | 32 lbs. Compound bow |
|---|---|
| 28<br>Beman ICS<br>Hunter Junior | 153 ft./sec. max. |
| 32<br>Beman ICS<br>Bowhunter | 144 ft./sec. max. |

**Table 10-2** Comparison of speeds of arrows shot from a compound bow.

Any measuring instrument has to be calibrated before use. The best way will be to have two instruments from different manufacturers measure the speed of an arrow at the same time. However, I do not have a second type of speed recorder.

In scientific studies, the conditions of speed measurements are done in a controlled environment. The arrows are released by machines. However, machines don't shoot in the backyard. Archers do. Hence, for recreational shooting the speeds recorded in Tables 10-1 and 10-2 are good enough as backyard information and will give the archer an idea of how fast an arrow travels.

# Trajectory of the Arrow

After the arrow is released and leaves the bowstring, it will trace a parabolic curve. The coordinates, the position of the arrow, at any time is shown as (x, y) in Figure A-3.

The x-coordinate, in terms of the time of flight $t$ is

$$x = (v_0 \cos A)\, t \qquad\qquad \textbf{(Equation 1)}$$

and the y-coordinate is

$$y = (v_0 \sin A)\, t - \tfrac{1}{2}gt^2. \qquad\qquad \textbf{(Equation 2)}$$

where A is the angle of release of the arrow.

At the same time that the arrow travels horizontally, it also travels vertically. Hence, the $t$ in Equation 1 is the same as the $t$ in Equation 2. We can solve for $t$ in the x equation (1) then substitute it in the y equation (2) yielding

$$y = x \tan A - \frac{g}{2v_0^2 \cos^2 A} \times^2 \qquad\qquad \textbf{(Equation 3)}$$

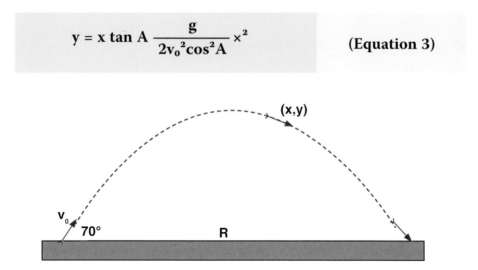

**Figure 10-2:** The position of the arrow in flight (Not to scale).

In the special case where y = 0, x = R, where R is the *range*, Equation 3 simplifies to

$$x = R = \frac{v_0^2}{g} \sin 2A \qquad\qquad \textbf{(Equation 4)}$$

The maximum distance the arrow could travel is when sin2A = 1, that is, when A = 45° above the horizontal.

We will use the range of velocities as measured with the speed detector to find this maximum distance. We will rewrite Equation 4, with A = 45°, sin2A = sin 90°

$$x = R = \frac{v_0^2}{g} \sin 90° \qquad \textbf{(Equation 5)}$$

where sin 90° = 1. Hence,

$$x = R = \frac{v_0^2}{g} (1) \qquad \textbf{(Equation 6)}$$

We will assume that the measured range of velocities 106 ft./sec.–126 ft./sec. is the range of initial velocities. The quantity g = 32.2 ft./sec. This gives

$$R = 349 \text{ ft.} - 493 \text{ ft.}$$

This further emphasizes the need for great care in shooting the bow for the arrow will travel beyond a small backyard. But there is a way to minimize such an overshoot. Place your target at ground level and provide a back stop for glancing hits.

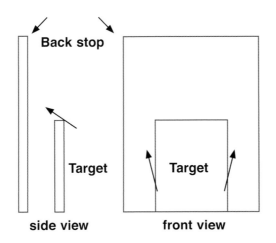

**Figure 10-3:** Your back stop should provide for glancing hits at the top and at the sides of the target.

If you shoot with no backstop (Figure 10-3), the arrow that glances off the top of the target might just get launched at 45°.

ARROW SPEED AND TRAJECTORY 101

For the curious reader, suppose the apex of the roof of your house is at 18" at what angle would an arrow be shot to clear the roof and end in somebody's backyard?

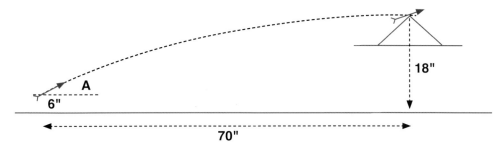

**Figure 10-4:** The arrow is released 6" off the ground at angle A (Not to scale).

We will rewrite equation 3

$$y = x \tan A - \frac{g}{2v_0^2 \cos^2 A} \times^2 \qquad \textbf{(Equation 3)}$$

Here, the given values are y = 12" (=18"– 6"), distance x = 70" and g is the universal constant 32.2 ft./sec. We will use $v_0$ = 126 ft./sec. Thus, we have one equation and one unknown, A. Substituting the given values into the y equation yields

$$5.8 \sin A \cos A - \cos^2 A = 0.42$$

It is not easy to solve for A. The only way I know is by trial and error. Assume a value for A until the left side of the equation equals 0.42. It took me five tries. A calculator will make the process a lot easier. Using this method, A = 14°.

You might be curious to know the maximum height you arrow could reach. This is easy enough to determine. The formula that applies is

$$h = (v_0)^2 \sin^2 A / 2g$$

The height "h" will be maximum when $\sin^2 A = 1$, that is when A = 90°. Hence,

$$h = (v_0)^2 / 2g$$

$$h = (126)^2 / 2(32) = 248 \text{ ft.}$$

This is not to encourage you to shoot upward. The arrow could very well land on your, or someone else's, head. Of course you are not going to shoot at 45°, at 14°, or vertically upward but at some smaller angles such as are shown in Figure 10-5 (not to scale).

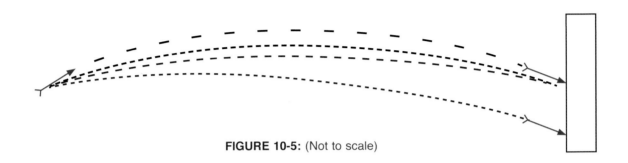

**FIGURE 10-5:** (Not to scale)

CHAPTER 11

# TRACKING YOUR PROGRESS

It is not necessary to track your progress. You might be satisfied with just hitting your target. However, if you want to keep track, you cannot rely on memory. It is doubtful if you can remember how well you did two months ago. Hence, it is better to keep written records of your shooting sessions. This can be done by counting hits and misses, grouping, scoring, or plotting a learning curve.

# Hit or Miss

You assign one point to an arrow that hits inside the target; zero, to one that hits outside. If you shoot 25 arrows each day, you can keep records of your hits and misses. When you shoot enough, you can make a comparison on a week by week, or a month by month basis. However, if you shoot 25 one day, 46 the next, and 100 the next day, you will have to use percentage hits to make a comparison. Figure 11-6 uses this method of tracking progress.

# Grouping

The concept of grouping can be better understood by looking at Figure 11-1. Figure 11-1A has a tighter group than Figure 11-1B. However, shooter B is more accurate than shooter A. Hence, grouping must be interpreted in relation to the center of the target.

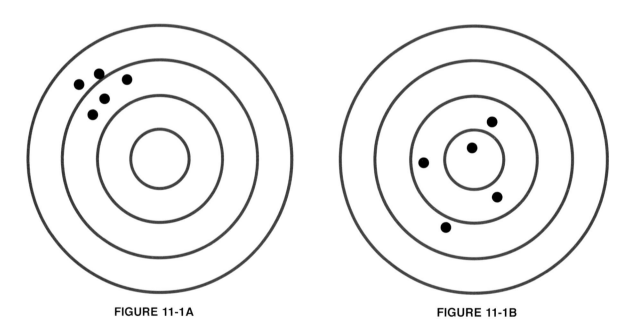

**FIGURE 11-1A**                          **FIGURE 11-1B**

**Figure 11-1A (above left) and Figure 11-1B (above right):** A dot represents the point of entry of an arrow.

# Scoring Points

In the martial arts, grouping will have no meaning. If a person is targeted with an arrow and gets hit, he is going down. But shooting at a human figure is useful because specific points can be targeted for points. Figure 11-2 (A and B) shows targets that are based on a human figure. Points are given for a hit on the head (10); on the 8½"×11" rectangular piece or 8" circle (5); on any other spot in the torso, (3).

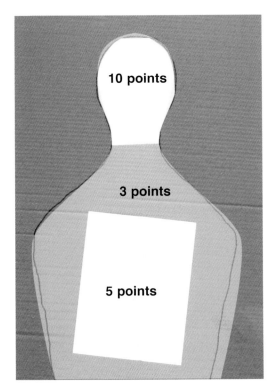
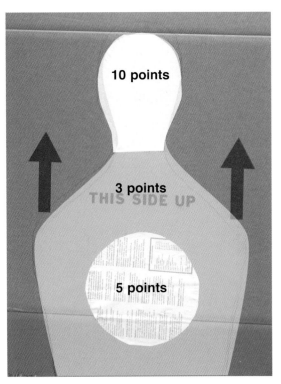

**FIGURE 11-2A (above left) and FIGURE 11-2B (above right):** Scoring your shots.

Table 11-1 lists my score for one hundred arrows shot in sets of ten. The maximum possible score is one hundred points. The best score (#10) is sixty five points. However, there were three missed shots. The missed shots were aimed at the head.

In time of conflict, these are three adversaries that could shoot back at the archer. Hence, it is better to aim at the torso (#1, #3, #4, #7, & #9) which is a bigger target than the head.

| Sets of ten | 3 points | | 5 points | | 10 points | | Missed shots | Total points |
|---|---|---|---|---|---|---|---|---|
| | Hits | Score | Hits | Score | Hits | Score | | |
| 2 | 1 | 3 | 6 | 30 | 2 | 20 | 1 | 53 |
| 3 | 2 | 6 | 8 | 40 | - | - | - | 46 |
| 4 | 3 | 9 | 7 | 35 | - | - | - | 44 |
| 5 | 1 | 3 | 4 | 20 | 3 | 30 | 2 | 53 |
| 6 | 2 | 6 | 5 | 25 | 3 | 30 | - | 61 |
| 7 | 2 | 6 | 8 | 40 | - | - | - | 46 |
| 8 | 1 | 3 | 9 | 45s | - | - | - | 48 |
| 9 | 3 | 9 | 7 | 35 | - | - | - | 44 |
| 10 | 0 | 0 | 1 | 5 | 6 | 60 | 3 | 65 |

**Table 11-1**: Scores for 100 shots in sets of ten. In archery competitions fewer arrows are used for each end (the sets of arrows shot in a competition). However, it is easier to keep track by shooting in groups of 10 or 5 when shooting alone.

Figure 11-3 (opposite page) shows a traditional target of concentric circles. The 2", 4", 6" and 8" concentric circles are assigned 5, 4, 3, 1 points respectively. I shot twenty arrows in sets of five. The maximum score is 20 × 5 (=100). In the first month, my average is 30%; in the 12th month, 91%. After the 12th month, I changed my target and discontinued plotting the learning curve. I had to change the target because I damaged several arrow nocks with "Robin Hood shots." (See Figure 4-8 and Figure 4-9 on page 50.)

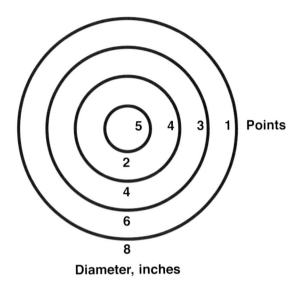

**Figure 11-3:** Scoring for a circular target with concentric circles.

Table 11-2 is an example of how to score your shots using the target shown in Figure 11-3. Each arrow has the maximum value of five points. Hence, if you shoot twenty arrows, the perfect score is 100. Here, the archer hit the bull's-eye two times. Only eighteen arrows hit inside the circles; two were misses and are scored zero. The score is 50 out of a possible 100 points.

| Diameter of circle, inch | Points | Shots | Score |
|:---:|:---:|:---:|:---:|
| 8 | 1 | 6 | 6 |
| 6 | 3 | 6 | 18 |
| 4 | 4 | 4 | 16 |
| 2 | 5 | 2 | 10 |
| Miss | 0 | 2 | 0 |
| Total | | 20 | 50 |

**Table 11-2:** How to score your shots using a circular target with concentric circles.

# Learning Curve

Another way of tracking your progress is by plotting your shooting average over a period of time. The resulting graph pictures what is known as the learning curve (Figure 11-4). The learning curve is a limited growth curve, meaning, learning cannot increase indefinitely. One will eventually reach his upper limit beyond which he can't progress anymore. In the language of mathematics, he would have reached his *horizontal asymptote*.

Should you decide to plot your learning curve, do not be limited by my percent average. You might do better than I did. You can use my learning curve as a point of reference. This way, even if you shoot alone, you will know how you are progressing compared to another archer.

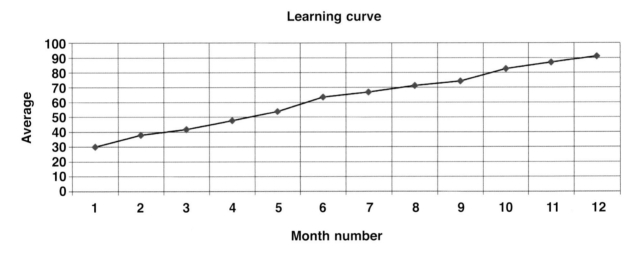

**Figure 11-4:** My learning curve shows steady progress over a period of twelve months. The curve can be drawn manually or generated by using Excel. This curve was generated using instinctive shooting, that is, no sight was attached to the bow. Shooting distance was 20 yards.

| Month Number | 1 | 2 | 3 | 4 | 5 | 6 | 7 | 8 | 9 | 10 | 11 | 12 |
|---|---|---|---|---|---|---|---|---|---|---|---|---|
| Average % | 30 | 38 | 42 | 48 | 54 | 64 | 67 | 71 | 74 | 83 | 87 | 91 |

**Table 11-3:** Monthly average percentage using the learning curve in Figure 11-4.

## Learning Curve Using a Sight

One of my students started shooting a left handed recurve without a sight. After several weekends of shooting she purchased a sight and provided a commentary of her experience.

- In instinctive shooting she shot the bow with both eyes open; with the sight, she shot with her right eye closed.
- In instinctive shooting, she pulled to her anchor point; with the sight, she pulled the bow string just short of the full draw, aimed using the sight and then pulled to her anchor point.
- In instinctive shooting, her breathing came naturally; with the sight, she had to control her breathing.
- In instinctive shooting, she did not feel fatigued after 5 arrow shots; with the sight, she did.
- In instinctive shooting, she used the close stance; with the sight, she shot in the open stance.
- It took her longer to shoot 5 arrows shooting with a sight.

**Figure 11-5A (left) and Figure 11-5B (above):** Shooting the recurve with a sight attached (Courtesy Thoraya Zedan).

Her hit percentage increased dramatically despite the adjustments she made. See Figure 11-6.

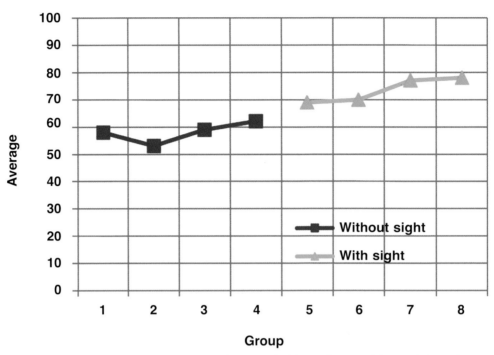

**Figure 11-6:** There was a dramatic increase in hit % after attaching a sight to the recurve bow.

| Hit % | Miss % | Group | Without sight (%) | With sight (%) |
|---|---|---|---|---|
| 58 | 42 | 1 | 58 | |
| 53 | 47 | 2 | 53 | |
| 59 | 41 | 3 | 59 | |
| 62 | 48 | 4 | 62 | |
| 69 | 31 | 5 | | 69 |
| 70 | 30 | 6 | | 70 |
| 77 | 23 | 7 | | 77 |
| 78 | 22 | 8 | | 78 |

**Table 11-4:** Hit percentage with and without a sight.

APPENDIX A

# PRACTICE GAMES

On a lighter note, here are two simple games that you can easily set up yourself. While they may seem simple, the point of these exercises is to have fun while getting in some valuable practice time. They are a great way to practice your instinctive shooting. You may even forget you are actually practicing!

# Tic-Tac-Toe

Figure A-1 shows a simple a set-up of nine circles that can be used to play a game of tic-tac-toe. You can easily attach the circles to one of your practice targets.

You can play alone to see how long it takes you to accurately hit the targets or you can play with an archer friend. If you play with a friend, you will need to mark your arrows. Red nail polish is a good marker.

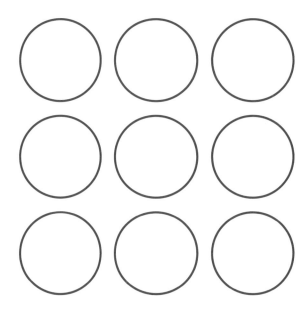

**Figure A-1:** A set of nine circles for a game of tic-tac-toe.

When playing the game, use the rules of tic-tac-toe—taking alternating shots, the first player to hit three circles in a row (diagonally, horizontally or vertically) wins the game. You should also decide on a shooting distance for each player. You can choose a distance that suits your ability or you can also choose a longer distance if you want a challenge.

# Lottery Numbers

Here is a fun game that is not dependent on hitting a specific target unless you really want to. Use the circle set-up below (Figure A-2) to create a target that will help you pick a lottery number (or any other number you want). If you created several targets for the tic-tac-toe game, you can use those with numbers added to the circles.

You can set up a cardboard target with nine 4" circles numbered from 1 to 9 (Figure A-2) and generate a set of numbers that you could play in the lottery. Place an imaginary 0 in each circle. For example: The circle numbered 1 can also be a 10. If you hit 1 with your first arrow and hit a 2 in your next arrow, you can have three numbers: 10, 20, or 12. You can take your pick.

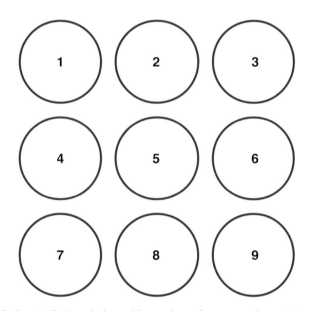

**Figure A-2:** A set of nine circles with numbers for generating a lottery number.

You can generate numbers with a friend taking turns to shoot. I played this game with one of my students but I haven't won anything, yet. Maybe you will have better luck than I did and then you can have a bigger backyard! One thing is for sure, though; you will be practicing your instinctive shooting while having fun.

# MAKING YOUR OWN BOW AND ARROW

A fun activity for anyone interested in archery is making your own bow and arrow. The result may not be as polished or as technologically advanced as your manufactured bow and arrow but it can work well and give you a connection to the past.

In order to make a bow and arrow, you will need a saw, files, a vise, a Dremel tool, sandpaper, work space, and a lot of patience. If you have a belt sander you can use it to put the finishing touches on the arrows and the bows. However, since the wood for the arrows and the bows are freshly cut, your sanding belt can easily get clogged. I opted not to use my belt sander. Instead, I used a carpet cutter to whittle the wood for the bows and for the arrows to the sizes and shapes needed.

# Making the Arrow

**Shaft**—Small tree branches can grow nearly straight. A freshly cut branch is pliable and can be made straight by bending against the knee (protected by a knee pad). Or you might need to soften it by heating it in an open flame or by using steam. If you use an open flame, wet the wood before heating it. It can be debarked then whittled to the final diameter that can be used as an arrow.

The center of gravity of the 29" carbon arrow is at 18½" from the nock. Meaning the arrow is front end heavy. (Note that in knife throwing, it is more comfortable to throw a knife when its center of gravity is at or past the finger tips – front end heavy.) There are two ways to have the center of gravity toward the front: put the nock or an arrow head on the thinner end. However, I made an arrow where its center of gravity is toward the nock end to check out how it will behave in flight. See Figure B-1.

Arrows can also be made from bamboo but you need one that is thick enough. In Virginia, where I live, what is called river cane is actually bamboo. They are not thick enough. Bamboo species that are (Figure B-7, extreme left) grow widely in Asia. We had that kind in my backyard when I was growing up.

The shafts in Figure B-1 were freshly cut and thus heavy. As the wood dries the shafts will become lighter.

**Fletchings**—I used a Dremel tool to cut the groove on the nock with a thicker grinding wheel than the one used to cut the 2" slit. I applied glue on the slit, inserted the fletchings and then applied more glue. It is really only a fletching since it is made of one piece. I cut it from transparent plastic that is used to cover table cloths. It is pliable enough to simulate commercial fletchings. You can also use a hacksaw to cut the groove.

I had only one feather to work with so I cut it in two. Thus, the top side of the feather shows in one (Figure B-1, the arrow on the extreme right) and in the other, the under side.

The arrows with the transparent plastic vanes shoot well from 20 yards in my commercial recurve. The feathered arrow shoots erratically with the bow shown in Figure B-9 which I attribute to the bent shaft.

**Figure B-1:** The centers of gravity of the arrows are located at the strip of yellow and green tapes. Second from left is a wooden arrow with the fletchings attached to the thin end thus putting the center of gravity closer to the arrow head. Third from left is one with the fletchings attached to the thick end thus putting the center of gravity is closer to the nock end. At the extreme right is a feathered arrow.

**Figure B-2:** There are many materials you can use for plastic vanes. Two possible sources I have used are a sheet protector (left) and an envelope for lottery tickets (right).

**Arrow rest**—Small twigs that have the shape of the arrow rest shown in Figure B-3 can be found in any tree. Privet is a good source. I made one and I attached it to the rattan bow with duct tape.

The first time I tried the improvised arrow rest (Figure B-3), I missed the target by the proverbial mile. The commercial arrow veered to the right. I snipped off part of the arrow rest then tightened the duct tape. A notch with a width of half the diameter of the arrow (Figure B-4) cut into the bow is a better arrow rest than the twig. With this dimension, the vanes will clear the ledge formed by the notch. If the branch is thick enough, the notch should not weaken the bow.

**Figure B-3:** Arrow rest made from privet.

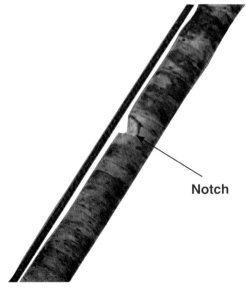

Notch

**Figure B-4:** A notch cut on the bow to make an arrow rest.

# Making the Bow

Rattan is an excellent material for making bows. Because it is commonly used to make furniture, it can easily be bent. There are many species of rattan. Some are heavy while some are light. Denser rattan would result in a bow that will require a greater pull. The rattan pictured (Figure B-4) is of the light variety and has less than a 15 lbs. pull.

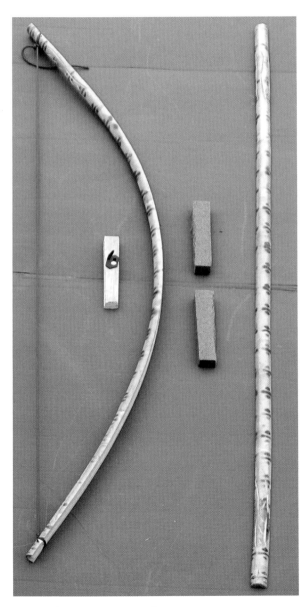

**Figure B-5:** A bow made from rattan that was cut in half along its length.

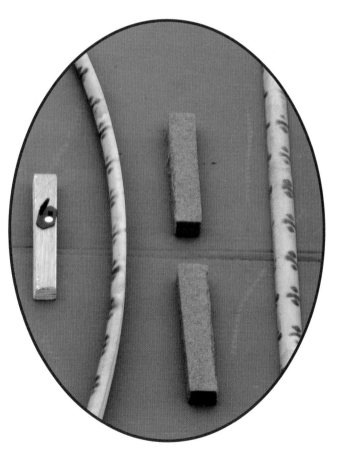

**Figure B-6:** A close-up of Figure B-5 shows the wood or Styrofoam pieces that can be attached to the bow's back onto which a commercial arrow rest can be glued.

Freshly cut bamboo can be easily trimmed then whittled to its final thickness and shape. On the other hand, palm wood such as the *bahi* (Figure B-7, right) will need more work because it is very dense. The *bahi* is used as flooring material because they have beautiful grains or posts because they are durable. If I remember right, there is a bow made from *bahi* displayed in the Smithsonian.

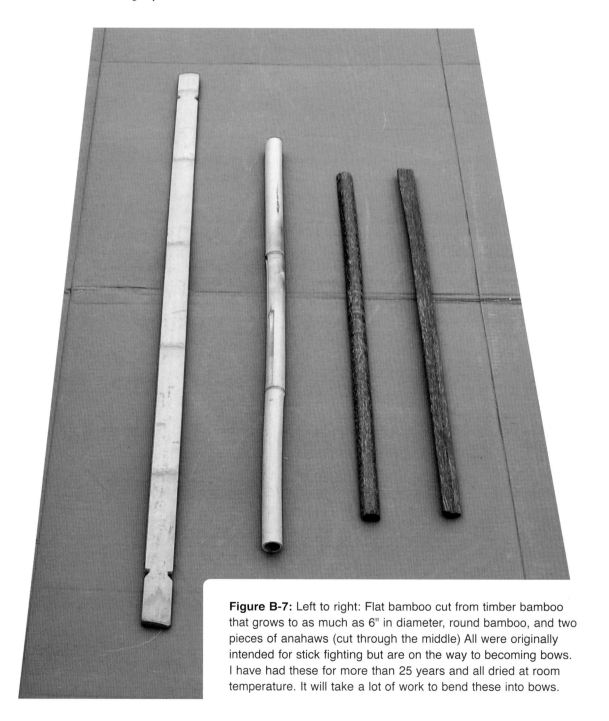

**Figure B-7:** Left to right: Flat bamboo cut from timber bamboo that grows to as much as 6" in diameter, round bamboo, and two pieces of anahaws (cut through the middle) All were originally intended for stick fighting but are on the way to becoming bows. I have had these for more than 25 years and all dried at room temperature. It will take a lot of work to bend these into bows.

A freshly cut tree branch can be bent easily (Figure B-8). I used a 550 paracord (which is about the size of the bowstring on my recurve) to link the limbs with the bow having a brace height of 6". It pulls less than 15 lbs. As it dries, the bow will acquire a permanent curve. When it has dried enough it will become stiff after which the limbs can then be bent to a brace height of 10" at which time it will require a pull greater than 15 lbs.

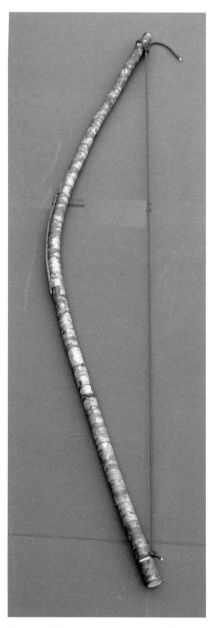

**Figure B-8:** Freshly cut wood.

**Figure B-9:** A bow can be made by simply bending a freshly cut tree branch. Here, a twig is attached using duct tape to the bow as the arrow rest.

# But will it Shoot Straight?

The bow must be of the proper weight to propel the arrow so it will get to the target. The bow shown in Figure B-9 pulls less than 15 lbs. I was able to hit the target from 25 feet using this bow and the arrows in Figure B-1—not consistently though for a number of reasons.

Arrows must be straight, of uniform weight, and match the bow in stiffness. Arrows made "quick and dirty" from tree branches are usually not straight (Figure B-1). They don't have uniform weights. The arrows' stiffness is as varied as the number of branches used.

One can compensate for the weight of an arrow by aiming at a higher elevation. However, trying to compensate for the left/right placement will be difficult since the arrow could be bent to the left and downward, or to the right and upward, or some other way. Since there are two vanes, the arrow can be nocked in two ways thus adding another set of variables to the flight characteristics of the arrow. One other variable added is the twig that served as an arrow rest (Figure B-10).

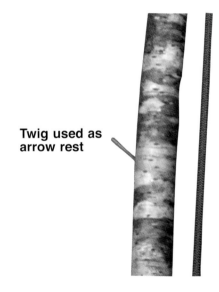

**Twig used as arrow rest**

**Figure B-10:** A close-up of a twig used as a simple arrow rest.

Despite these variables, I was able to hit my target (using my recurve) with the wooden arrows shown in Figure B-1 (above) from 20 yards. However, I have still to wait for the bow in Figure B-7 to dry and become stiff enough so that it can propel an arrow with a weight greater than 15 lbs.

Table B-1 shows a summary in matrix format of how my self-made bow fared against my commercial recurve.

| Arrow type | Homemade bow | Commercial recurve |
|---|---|---|
| Wooden arrow | Inconsistent hitting % | Shoots well |
| Commercial arrow | Inconsistent hitting % | Shoots well as expected |

**Table B-1**: Results of shooting a homemade bow vs. a commercial recurve.

I had fun making the nocks and will grade myself a B. I also had fun constructing the arrows and will grade myself a C. In all, I believe that making your own bow and arrow is an enjoyable exercise and, if you are truly interested in archery, will be both an entertaining and educational project.

# GLOSSARY

*Anchor (low)*—final position (before the release) of the string hand where the "V" formed by the index finger and thumb is placed under the jaw and where the bow string touches the tip of the nose and the chin.

*Anchor (high)*—final position (before the release) of the string hand where the thumb's knuckle is held against the cheek.

*Anchor (classic)*—the same as high anchor.

*Anchor (western)*—the same as low anchor.

*Arm guard (also called bracer)*—a strap of leather or canvas that protects the bow arm from getting hit by the string.

*Arrow*—consists of the arrow head, insert, hollow or solid shaft, fletchings, and nock.

*Bow, compound*—a bow where the energy of pull is transmitted by a system of cables and cams to and stored in the limbs.

*Bow, long*—a bow where the tips of the limbs point toward the archer.

*Bow, recurve*—a bow where the tips of the limbs point away from the archer.

*Bow hand/arm*—the hand/arm that holds the bow.

*Bow press*—a devise used to press limbs of the compound bow toward the center to take tensions off the bowstring and cables to do maintenance work on compound bows such as changing the bowstring.

*Bow string*—the string that connects the two limbs of the bow.

*Brace height* (or *fistmele*)—the distance from the grip to the bowstring.

*Cams*—pulleys used in compound bows.

*Clicker*—a device that clicks when the archer reaches his optimum draw length.

*Cock feather* (or *index fletching*)—one of the three vanes made of feathers or plastic attached close to the end of the arrow shaft oriented perpendicular to the bowstring that has a different color than the other two.

*Dominant eye*—right eye dominant archers usually hold the bow with left hand.

*Drawing hand* or *string hand*—the hand that draws the string.

*Dry firing*—**unsafe and not recommended** releasing of the bow string without a nocked arrow.

*End*—a number of arrows shot during archery competitions.

*Finger tab*—a piece of leather worn over the 3 middle fingers to allow the smooth release of the bowstring.

*Fletchings*—the three or more feathers or plastic vanes that stabilize the arrow in flight.

*Full draw*—a draw where the string hand is pulled to the anchor point.

*Index fletching* (or *cock feather*)—one of the three vanes made of feathers or plastic attached close to the end of the arrow shaft oriented perpendicular to the bowstring that has a different color than the other two.

*Instinctive shooting*—a style of shooting without the aid of a mechanical or fixed sight.

*Group*—a measure of consistency that refers to the closeness of the embedded arrows to each other.

*Kisser*—a button or a bump on the bow string which, upon contact with the puckered lips of a low-anchor archer, indicates that he has anchored correctly.

*Nock (arrow)*—grooved plastic attached to the shaft's end.

*Nock* (bow)—notch at the ends of the bow where the ends of the bow string are looped.

*Nocking point*—space between the string nocks.

*Nocks (string)*—pair of small C shaped metal attached to the string between which the arrow is nocked.

*Over bowed*—a condition where an archer tries to use a bow that requires a pull beyond his arm strength.

*Quiver*—containers used to carry arrows.

*Riser*—the middle section of the bow to which the limbs are attached.

*Robin Hood shot*—a shot that hits the nock of an already-embedded arrow.

*Serving*—nylon thread wrapped around the center of the bowstring that protects the strand from abrasion caused by the repeated nocking of the arrow; also wrapped around each end of the bowstring.

*Shooting glove*—a glove worn over the index, middle, and ring fingers that allows the smooth release of the bowstring and that protects the fingers from being rubbed raw.

*Snap shooting*—releasing the arrow too quickly before having taken careful aim.

*Spine* (static)—a measure of the stiffness of an arrow determined by hanging a static load of 1.94 lbs. at the middle of a 29" shaft supported ½" from each end.

*Spine* (dynamic)—deformation of the arrow that depends on many of factors among including the bow's draw weight, arrow weight of the arrow, weight of the inserts, method of release, and static spine.

*Stabilizer*—a device that reduces the twist of the bow as the string is released.

*Stance* (close)—a shooting position where the feet are parallel to each other.

*Stance* (open)—a shooting position of the feet where the front is at a slight angle to the other foot that is parallel to the target.

*String hand/arm*—the hand/arm that pulls the string.

*Tackle* – the archer's equipment.

*Vanes (fletchings)*—thin plastic material in shape of a parabola or feathers that stabilizes an arrow in flight.

# BIBLIOGRAPHY

Barker, Juliet. *Agincourt*. New York: Little Brown and Company, 2005.

Beman Arrows, http://beman.com.

Compound Bow Source, http://bestcompoundbowsource.com/

Gillelan, G. Howard. *Archery*. New York: Cornerstone Library, 1962.

Gross, W. H. (Chip). *Shooting & Archery*. Minneapolis, MN: Creative Publishing International, 2009.

Henderson, Al, and Dave Staples. *Peak Performance Archery*. Ft. Wayne, IN: Blue-J, Inc., 1987.

Lacy, Robert. *Great Tales from English History*. New York: Little Brown & Company, 2004.

Lancaster Archery Supply, http://www.lancasterarchery.com.

Mariñas I, Amante P. *Blowgun Techniques*. Rutland, VT: Tuttle Publishing, 2012.

_____. *The Art of Throwing*. Rutland, VT: Tuttle Publishing, 2010.

Realtree, https://www.realtree.com.

Shooting Time, http://shootingtime.com/

60X Custom Strings, http://www.60xcustomstrings.com.

The Art of Manliness, http://www.artofmanliness.com.

Twin Coast Archery Club, http://www.twincoastarchers.com.

University of Iowa, Office of the State Archaeologist. *American Indian Archery Technology*. https://archaeology.uiowa.edu/american-indian-archery-technology-0.

*Webster's New Twentieth Century Dictionary*. New York: Simon & Schuster, 1979.

Wikipedia, http://www.wikipedia.com.

# PHOTO CREDITS

Cherry D. Mariñas
Amante D. Mariñas II
Thoraya Zedan
Amante P. Mariñas I

www.flickr.com/search/?text=1883551633 by theremission

# ALSO BY THE AUTHOR

*Arnis de Mano* (with Porferio S. Lanada)
*Arnis Lanada: Master Filipino Combat Stick Fighting Tactics*
*The Art of Throwing: The Definitive Guide to Thrown Weapons Techniques*
*Blowgun Techniques: The Definitive Guide to Modern and Traditional*
  *Blowgun Techniques*
*Pananandata Dalawang Yantok: Two Stick Fighting*
*Pananandata: The Guide to Balisong Openings* (with Amante Mariñas, II)
*Pananandata: History and Techniques of the Daga, Yantok, Balisong, and Other*
  *Traditional Weapons of the Philippines*
*Pananandata Guide to Knife Throwing*
*Pananandata Guide to Sport Blowguns*
*Pananandata Knife Fighting*
*Pananandata Rope Fighting: Filipino Choking and Binding Techniques*
*Pananandata Yantok at Daga: Filipino Stick and Dagger*

# ABOUT THE AUTHOR

Amante P. Mariñas I grew up in Pambuan, a village with one road, no tap water and no electricity in Gapan, Nueva Ecija, in Central Luzon in the Philippines. He is a former professor of chemical engineering at Adamson University in Manila, Philippines, and holds black belts in aikido from the Philippine Aikido Club under Sensei Ambrosio Gavileno and in shorin-ryu from the Commando Karate Club under Sensei Latino Gonzalez and Sensei Anselmo "Pop" Santos. He trained briefly with Sifu Benito Coo in the snake form of kung fu.

Introduced to *pananandata*, a system of stick, knife, and empty hands fighting, by his granduncle Ingkong Leon Marcelo at the age of eight, Mariñas later expanded its scope and formally founded pananandata's expanded version in 1988. Mariñas has written thirteen books on pananandata. He designed a throwing knife marketed by United Cutlery that carries his name and was inducted into the International Knife Throwers Hall of Fame (IKTHOF) in October 2010. He is honorary chairman of the International Fukiyado Association based in Nagaoka, Japan.

Mariñas lives in Fredericksburg, Virginia. His wife of 46 years, Cherry, passed away on November 11, 2018. He has two grandchildren, Amante III and Nadia, born to his only child Amante II and TaShana Foreman-Mariñas. Amante II is heir to pananandata.